The LIFE Plan

Volume Six
Your Part in the Story

By Allen L. Elder

DEDICATION

The LIFE Plan in its entirety is dedicated to the members of Bethany Baptist Church of Spartanburg, South Carolina where the material was written and used for the very first time.

Table of Contents

INTRODUCTION

When I was six years old, I was born again into the family of God and became a follower of the Lord Jesus Christ. Almost immediately, I knew that I wanted to be in the ministry. For the next several years, I attended church and learned many facts about God and the Bible. However, I did not learn what to do with all of that information. No one intentionally and strategically discipled me into the purpose of God for my life. Frustrated by years of learning with no practical guidance, I walked away from the church. Another ten years went by before God put a leader in front of me who invited me to follow him as he followed Christ.

After twenty years of being a Christian, I was of not much use to the cause of Christ. After high school and the USAF, I started going to church with my girlfriend who later became my wife. It was then that God put some key people before me who taught me and led me with purpose. It made all the difference and I began to get some real traction in my life. Now, more than thirty years of ministry later, I can share The LIFE Plan with you to help you on your journey.

The LIFE Plan is a discipleship curriculum which takes you from a beginning with God into a life lived according to his purpose and for his glory. From it you will gain a grasp on the story and structure of the Bible, and on the Bible's strategy of spiritual reproduction and multiplication. You will also learn how to discover God's purpose for your own life so that you can serve him in the way he has designed you to serve.

The LIFE Plan is made up of six volumes containing 216 total lessons. Each lesson has a short text followed by a lesson outline, Scripture references, pathways for deeper study, and with questions which underscore the important truths from the lessons that you will need to know and understand. Some questions ask for your personal response which will help you to apply the material in your own life. The lessons are structured in the following way.

Volume One - The Bible's Story (Genesis 1-11)
Volume Two - The Bible's Story (Genesis 12- Malachi)
Volume Three - The Structure of the Entire Bible
Volume Four - The Life of Christ on Earth
Volume Five - The Church
Volume Six - Your Personal Ministry

With The LIFE Plan, you will be equipped with a knowledge of the Bible that will help you find your way through life. With the materials in hand, you will also be equipped to guide another person and other people to find their way as well. In so doing, you will be investing your life into others in fulfilment of the Lord's great commission to make disciples of all nations. Living your life intentionally in this way will indeed prepare you for eternity where you will give an accounting of what you did with that which God gave you on earth. If you are as I am, when the day comes when I stand before God, I will want to have lived my life on earth with eternity in mind.

The LIFE Plan is intended to be a curriculum from which you can learn and with which you can teach another disciple. There is no limit to what can be done with these lessons. They can be used in a variety of ways and for a variety of ministries. Following are some suggested ways to use the material.

1. Children's Ministry
2. Youth Ministry
3. Sunday School
4. Small Groups
5. Prison Ministry
6. Personal Discipling
7. Correspondence Course
8. In School and After School Programs
9. Sports Ministries
10. Missions
11. Bible Schools
12. Personal Study
13. Family Devotions
14. Online Studies

Our hope is that you will use these studies to reproduce reproducing disciples of Christ around the world. And we would love to hear about how you will use them. May God bless you as you learn and grow and invest into the lives of others.

Allen L. Elder

1. SALVATION

THEME: IN A NUT SHELL

BLOCK 6 - THEME 1 - LESSON 1

LESSON AIM: To give a clear presentation of the gospel of Jesus Christ.

This final year of your L.I.F.E. journey in discipleship is going to be focused on what you will do with your training for the rest of your life. You have been given the basics from the Bible which will help you continue to build, grow, serve, and become all that God wants you to be. The first four lessons this year are giving you, in a nut shell, what Christians ought to be concerned with: salvation, spiritual growth, your personal ministry, and evangelism. This basic overview will help us to keep ourselves on the right track of being involved in the important things in life. It will also guide us toward working to involve other people in the same process. Let's start by talking about salvation.

The created world is a beautiful thing. We have all seen wondrous beauty among the heavenly hosts of outer space, in the skies around our planet, from the ocean depths, and on the landscape itself. Everywhere we look there is a masterpiece in motion of creative beauty all around us.

Perhaps the most breathtaking beauty of all is found in the plain sight of daily life. It is so obvious and prevalent that we easily miss it. I am speaking of the beauty that is seen in all the peoples of the earth; the beauty of the family of mankind.

One of the most beautiful things about the nations is seen in their diversity. From some 12,000 people groups (depending upon whose groupings you read) no two of them are exactly alike. They each have those unique traits that set them apart from all the other peoples of the world. Each group has its own roots, traditions, and world view. The sum total of all these unique traits we think of as their culture.

While there are these unique traits that distinguish all the groups from the others, there are also some universal truths that can be found at the heart of every ethnic group. These are the things that are found in every group regardless of whom they are or where we may find them. These are the things that create common ground between the diverse nations of the earth. The universal truths we will address in this lesson are some of the ones we find that are of a spiritual nature. We will think of three of them.

When we hear the word "sin" we usually think of it in terms of the things we do. We think of sin as doing something bad or wrong on the shallow end and as something evil or unspeakable on the deepest end. While most of us realize we are not perfect, it is still sometimes hard even to admit that we have a problem with sin. We think of it in the lives of others perhaps as those things done on the deep end of the scale and for ourselves, those things on the shallow end. We think of ourselves as not being all that bad especially when we are compared with someone else. As long as we can think of our sin problem in this way, we can find it easy to dismiss the situation entirely from our lives. Our conclusion is that we are not that bad of a person and the things we do are not as bad as those things done by others so we are probably in pretty good shape, spiritually speaking that is.

There is another way to consider the matter of the sin problem. Instead of thinking of it initially in terms of the things we do, we need to think of it as a condition into which we are born. The wrong things we do are done not simply because we are bad people but because we find ourselves in a bad condition. And the bad condition we are in is that we have inherited a sin problem from Adam, the very first man to walk on the earth. He was the representative of the human race when he disobeyed God in the Garden of Eden (Genesis 1-3), and the sin he committed was charged to all of us. In the sight of God, we all have sinned against him. The Bible says it like this: "Therefore, as by the offense of one judgment came upon all men to condemnation" (Romans 5:18a).

When we begin to examine this condition we are in, we find that it is a terrible condition in which to be. The sin problem that we inherited from Adam has caused each one of us to die spiritually. In fact, this is the very thing that God said would happen if Adam ate from the tree that had been forbidden. God said, "In the day that you eat thereof, you will die" (Genesis 2:17). The death he was speaking of was a spiritual death. And the spiritual death was passed on to each one of us: "for as in Adam all die" (1 Corinthians 15:22a). In the New Testament, Paul spoke of us as being "dead in trespasses and in sins" (Ephesians 2:1). So the sin problem we inherited from Adam means that sin has caused us to die spiritually.

Spiritual death means that we are separated from God. The relationship man once had with God has been broken. Man no longer walks and talks with God in an up-close, personal relationship. Because of sin, man is alienated from God and is a stranger and an enemy to him. Man cannot see things from God's point of view. He cannot understand the things of God and has no understanding of his ways. Man is found to be without God and without hope apart from him (Ephesians 2:12).

To further complicate the matter, we are unable to come back to God on our own (Ephesians 2:8-9). After all, what can one do that is dead? We are unable to do anything by way of good works that would get us out of the desperate situation we are in before God. We cannot do anything or offer anything that would change God's mind toward us concerning the sin problem we have inherited from Adam. As God sees it, we are in a hopeless situation, unable to lift as much as a little finger to even contribute to our rescue from this separation from God.

Is there a way out of this condition of sin and separation from God? Can we be restored so that we can know God, and have a right relationship with him again? Yes, there is a solution! The Bible calls this the good news. It is good news because the situation we are in is the bad news. We are estranged from God and cannot come back to him on our own. We need a solution for our sin problem that will be acceptable to God on his terms. He himself has provided the solution we need and the solution is Jesus Christ. Jesus is the Son of God who came to the earth to lay down his life as a sacrifice in order to remove our problem of sin and the resulting separation from God that sin has caused. He shed his blood for us and died in our place that he might atone for our sin and reconcile us to God. He was buried and arose from the dead, proving that he was the Son of God and therefore qualified to die such a death on our behalf. This death, burial, and resurrection is the gospel, or good news, of the Lord Jesus Christ. This is the solution God has provided to bring us back into a relationship with him.

The death of Jesus is acceptable to God for our sin problem. John wrote that his death satisfied God's just and righteous demands concerning our sin (1 John 2:2a). We are unable to satisfy God for our sin, but Jesus was able, and he did all that was necessary to restore us to a right relationship with God. In the same way that Adam's sin was charged to each one of us, Jesus died for us so that his righteousness could be charged to those who believe on him and receive him in their heart. We have no righteousness of our own. The righteousness of Christ is the grounds of our new standing before God, even as much as if we had never even sinned at all.

Concerning the death of Jesus Christ and his righteousness that he transfers to us which covers, or blots out our sin before God, there is no other solution that God will accept. The name of Jesus is the only name in which we can come to God and receive his complete forgiveness and restoration (Acts 4:12). Jesus himself said, "I am the way, the truth, and the life: no man comes to the Father, but by me" (John 14:6). There is a single solution for our sin problem, and the solution is Jesus Christ. Only this solution is acceptable to God.

A story is told in the Old Testament of a great man who had been stricken with leprosy (2 Kings 5). A prophet of God told him that he could be made clean if he would dip himself seven times in the Jordan River. He was a proud man and did not want to follow the way in which God had prescribed his cleansing. He wanted to be made whole on his own terms. He went away from the prophet still covered with leprosy. His servants came to him and convinced him to swallow his pride and do as the man of God had said. He did, and he was cleansed of the disease of leprosy.

We can be cleansed of our sin problem in the same way that Naaman was cleansed of leprosy; by coming to God in the way that he has prescribed and in the way that is acceptable unto him. This way is through Jesus Christ. We can have our problem with sin dealt with once and for all, and have a right relationship with God through the work that Jesus has done on our behalf.

How can we have this wonderful experience? We can have a new life in Christ by believing on Jesus and receiving him in our heart, and by confessing with our mouth that he is the Messiah and that we are his follower (Romans 10:9-10). We can be proud, like Naaman, and try other ways to be cleansed of our sin, none of which will be acceptable to God. Or, we can come God's prescribed way, by grace through faith in the Lord Jesus Christ and have our relationship with God restored (Ephesians 2:8-9). It only makes sense to come to God in the way that he accepts so that we might be made new in his sight. "If any man is in Christ, he is a new creature: old things are passed away and all things become new" (2 Corinthians 5:17).

At The LIFE Network, we care about you. We want you to have a right relationship with God. This is the reason we have shared this good news with you. After reading and hearing this lesson, if something within you seems to be in agreement with what you have heard, I want to invite you to believe on Jesus Christ in your heart, confess him with your mouth, and receive a new life in him. I invite you to pray from your heart the following prayer to God, confessing your trust in Jesus for his salvation. Please pray these words to God.

"Dear God. I admit my separation from you because of my sin against you. I acknowledge that you sent Jesus to bring me back to you. I believe in my heart that Jesus is the Son of God. I believe that he died for me and that he arose from the dead. I

confess Jesus as Lord and Savior of my life. I repent of my sins. I receive your gift of salvation through Jesus Christ. Thank you for making me right with you. Amen."

If you prayed this prayer sincerely to God from your heart, you are now a child of God and are a part of his family. God is now your Father. We are your brothers and sisters in Christ. God wants you to grow in your relationship with him. He is working to get this same message to other people throughout the world and he has a job for you to do for him in this work. We want to help you discover what it is that he wants you to do and help you learn how to do it. Remember, as you begin to learn and grow in Christ, we are here for you to answer any of your questions and to help you along the way. Congratulations on your new relationship with God. We believe he has great things in store for you.

SALVATION
BLOCK 6 - THEME 1 - LESSON 1 (181 OF 216)
LESSON OUTLINE

Spiritual truths common to all peoples:

I EVERY PERSON HAS INHERITED A SIN PROBLEM FROM ADAM
Sin can be thought of as:
A. The things we do
    1. Not so bad things
    2. Very bad things
B. A condition into which we are born
    1. Spiritually dead
    2. Separated from God
    3. Unable to come to God on our own

II WE NEED A SOLUTION FOR OUR SIN PROBLEM THAT GOD WILL ACCEPT
A. The solution is Jesus Christ
    1. His death and burial
    2. His resurrection
B. God accepts the death of Christ in exchange for our sin
    1. Christ is the propitiation for our sin
    2. God accepts no other offering

III THROUGH JESUS WE CAN HAVE A RIGHT RELATIONSHIP WITH GOD
A. Come to God on God's terms
B. Believe on Christ and be saved

SCRIPTURES TO BROADEN YOUR UNDERSTANDING
1. Sin
   Romans 3:23
   Romans 6:23
   Ephesians 3:1-3

2. All sinned in Adam
   1 Corinthians 15:22

3. Salvation
   Ephesians 2:8-9
   Romans 10:9-10
   John 1:12
   John 5:24

4. The created world
   Genesis 1-2
   Romans 1:20
   Hebrews 11:1-3

LINES OF THEOLOGICAL CONNECTION
1. SIN
   Sin
   Inherited sin
   Man's depravity

2. SOTERIOLOGY
   Atonement
   Imputed righteousness
   Redemption
   Propitiation
   Salvation by grace

LESSON GLOSSARY
1. Inherit
   To receive from one's ancestors.

2. Condemnation
   The state of being declared guilty of wrong.
3. Atone
   To make amends; to set right.

4. Reconcile
   To cause to be friendly or harmonious again.

SALVATION
BLOCK 6 - THEME 1 - LESSON 1 (181 OF 216)
QUESTIONS

1. What are some beautiful sights you have seen in the created world?

2. Name some things that you enjoy about people.

3. Do you know your own ethnic background?

4. List some of the ethnic groups in your community.

5. Sin is devastating, not simply because of the things we do, but because of the condition into which we are born. List three results of our sinful condition.

6. What is the only solution God will accept for our sin problem?

7. How does God's solution for our sin problem come to us?

8. Jesus died on the cross for our sins and he arose from the dead. The Bible calls this the gospel, or good news. List two ways that God moves us to respond to the gospel.

9. Have you believed on Jesus for salvation?

10. Would you like to speak with someone about your decision to trust Christ?

2. SPIRITUAL GROWTH

THEME: IN A NUT SHELL

BLOCK 6 - THEME 1 - LESSON 2

LESSON AIM: Show that once we are saved, we need to grow spiritually.

When we are brought into a brand new relationship with God, we are as a new baby when it is born into the world (1 Peter 2:2). It is alive and well but completely dependent upon another human being to care for it until it matures enough to begin to take care of itself.

We have a similar situation in our lives when we begin to have children. When we bring them home from the hospital, we have to do everything for them. We have to feed them, bathe them, clothe them, teach them to walk and talk, and everything else. Eventually, they become capable of doing these things for themselves. The goal is that one day they will be able to do these things for their own children. This is how it is with new Christians. They have to grow in order to become more than they are when they are born again into God's family.

There are a number of ways that Christians refer to this process of spiritual growth. We call it growing in Christ, spiritual growth, spiritual development, maturing in Christ, and discipleship, among other things. Any one of these phrases or words refers to the same process. I personally like the term, discipleship. Before believers in God were called Christians, they were called disciples. A disciple is a learner and a follower. This definition encompasses our maturing process as well as the work we are to do for God as his followers in the world.

If a child is going to grow, he is going to have to eat. He must have a regular intake of nourishing food that will cause his physical development to take place as it should. Christians, or disciples, also need nourishing food in order to grow spiritually. The food that has been provided for our spiritual development is the Bible, God's holy word. Let's see how the Bible can help us in the process of spiritual growth and development that we might become more than we are now for the glory of God.

The Bible is not an ordinary book. In fact, it is the most unusual book in the history of the world. The thing that makes it so unusual is that it was given to us by God himself. The Bible claims for itself that it is inspired by God (2Timothy 3:16). That is, the words we are given are from the mind and mouth of God, written for us by human authors (2Peter 1:21).

The Bible was written over a period of about 1,500 years by about 40 different men. It does not tell us everything about God. It says that the world itself could not contain the books that should be written about Jesus (John 21:25). It does tell us however, enough to know that God created us, loves us, cares for us, and has done everything necessary to make us at one with him again. It tells us how to know him in an intimate way. And, it tells us enough that pertains to life and to godliness that will make it possible for us to live lives that will be pleasing to God. The information the Bible contains on these and other subjects is the food we need in order to grow spiritually.

Since the Bible is of a spiritual nature, it requires that we interact with it on a spiritual level. Spiritual things must be spiritually discerned (1Corinthians 2:14). As we interact with the word of God, we are actually interacting with God himself. The same Holy Spirit who inspired the Bible can give us the illumination we need to receive it, understand it, and apply it in our lives (Ephesians 1:17-19). Therefore when we come to read the Bible, we must come humbly and dependent upon God to help us as we read. If we come to God and the Scriptures in a proud and haughty way, or in a rebellious way, he will withhold his illumination and see that we do not get what we need from the Bible. The attitude of our heart toward God and his word conditions his response toward us in the matter of understanding the Bible. As we come to the word, we need to ask God to correct any wrong attitude within our heart and let us receive his wisdom as we read his word (1Peter 5:5-7).

The Bible was given to us that we might grow from the reading, study, and living of it. For the baby Christian, the Bible is like milk to a little baby. It has in it everything that baby Christian needs for his growth and development as an infant, to a toddler, to a child. For the maturing Christian, the same Bible is like meat that will help him develop into a strong adult for the Lord's use (Hebrews 5:13-14). In this way, the Bible can help us become much more than we are now as we learn and follow that which God reveals to us in the Bible.

There are many things that help us along the way in our spiritual growth. Among those things are Christian friends and mentors, the church, a pastor, a small group, books and other tools for the study of the Bible. The one thing that will help us the most to grow spiritually is the Bible itself. As we begin to get into the Bible, we find that in the process, the Bible, or God's word, is getting into us. By getting into us, we begin to see life and to approach life from God's point of view which is presented to us in the Bible. Before long, we are applying the Word of God to our life in the decisions that we are making and are seeking to live life after the patterns God is revealing to us from the Bible.

2 Timothy 3:16-17 names four ways the Bible helps us in our spiritual growth. It says the Scriptures are profitable to us for doctrine, reproof, correction and instruction. Through these ministries of the Word, we mature and become equipped to do the work God has for us to do.

When we read the Word, we should try to determine these four works in the Scriptures with which we are reading. Doctrine is the body of truth which lies at the foundation of our belief. What we believe conditions how we behave. Through doctrine, God reveals his ways to us, showing us his standards which should govern our lives. Reproof is the work of the Scriptures which addresses the wrong belief or wrong behavior in which we are engaged. When the Scripture reproves us, it is telling us that either we believe something that is wrong, or we are going against a correct doctrine, or teaching, that we believe. Correction is when the Bible tells us how to fix something that is wrong. And, instruction from the Word is that which helps us stay on course. In brief, the Bible tells us what is right; what is wrong; how to make it right; and how to keep it right. As God does this work within us through the Scriptures, we can experience spiritual growth.

The only way the Bible is going to be able to help us is by our using it on a regular basis. The first thing we have to do is to read it (Colossians 4:16). Of course, the Bible can be an intimidating book, hard to read and understand. But the more we read it and get to know it, the more enjoyable it becomes to read it and to learn more from it. We have to discipline ourselves to spend some time taking in God's Word. There is no substitute for it whatsoever.

Next, as we read the Bible, we have to believe it (Hebrews 11:6). We have to take God at his word. We cannot believe it and reject it at the same time. There will be parts of it that we will have to wrestle with, but this is alright. The wrestling will help us consider all the angles and know why we believe the Word. This in turn will equip us to explain things to other people who are wrestling with the same issues.

We have to study the Bible (2Timothy 2:15). The Bible is a very simple book on the one hand and very complex on the other hand. It has a unique structure that is revealing in itself as to how God works in our lives. Each book of the Bible has a structure that helps us in conjunction with its message to unfold the meaning of the book as God intended it. The study of the bible should be our life-long endeavor.

We should discuss our findings in the Bible with other people (Colossians 3:16). This will help us as well as them. The insight that we gain through our study of the Bible will help others to grow as we share it with them. It will also prepare the way for us to receive more light upon God's Word as we continue to study it. Perhaps some insight another person has will be the key to opening new doors for our understanding and growth also.

Finally, we must apply God's Word to our lives every day (Psalms 119:33). We must learn to live by it. It is not enough to have a bunch of facts about the Bible and about God. The point is that in knowing these facts they help us to walk with God and live in his ways and to do the work he has planned for us to do while we are here on earth. The Bible is the most important tangible thing we have to help us live life in a way that is acceptable to God.

It is a blessing from God to have a church in our communities. The local church building provides the people of God with a base from which to operate as we do the work God has instructed us to do throughout the world. The church, as we have already seen, tells us how to have a right relationship with God. It also tells us how to become more than we are now by use of the Bible which is the key to our spiritual growth.

The LIFE Network wants to help you make progress in your life and ministry for God. We want to help you experience the difference God can make in your life through the Bible that he has given to us. Would you be willing to make a commitment to read and study the Bible? Would you be willing to let us show you the way to do this? Let's tell God about this decision in prayer.

"Heavenly Father. Thank you for your Word. Thank you that you moved toward us by giving us this word so that we can know you, live for you, and help others to do the same. With your help, I commit to read and study your word. Help me to get into it. Help me to grow spiritually. Help me to become more than I am now. Help me to become all that you want me to be for your glory. In Jesus name I pray. Amen."

SPIRITUAL GROWTH
BLOCK 6 - THEME 1 - LESSON 2 (182 OF 216)
LESSON OUTLINE

I THE BIBLE IS OUR KEY FOR SPIRITUAL GROWTH
    A. No ordinary book
        1. Comes from God
        2. Inspired by God
    B. The writing of the Bible
        1. All about God
        2. How to know God
        3. How to live for God
    C. The Bible is spiritually discerned
        1. God can conceal the truth
        2. God can reveal the truth

II HOW DOES SPIRITUAL GROWTH TAKE PLACE THROUGH USE OF THE BIBLE?
Four ways the Bible helps us grow spiritually
    A. Doctrine
    B. Reproof
    C. Correction
    D. Instruction

III WHAT SHOULD WE DO TO GROW SPIRITUALLY?
    A. Read it
    B. Believe it
    C. Study it
    D. Discuss it
    E. Apply it

SCRIPTURES TO BROADEN YOUR UNDERSTANDING
1. Christians
   First called disciples (Acts 11:26)

2. Spiritual Food
   Hebrews 5:13-14

3. God's Word to us
   3 Peter 1:3-4

4. God's Word in us
   Colossians 3:16

LINES OF THEOLOGICAL CONNECTION
1. BIBLIOLOGY
   Inspiration of the Scriptures
   Illumination
   Revelation
   The Bible writers
   Canonization of the Scriptures
   Using Bible study tools

2. PNEUMATOLOGY
   Discernment

3. ANTHROPOLOGY
   Spiritual growth

LESSON GLOSSARY
1. Inspiration
   God-breathed

2. Reproof
   To address a fault

SPIRITUAL GROWTH
BLOCK 6 - THEME 1 - LESSON 2 (182 OF 216)
QUESTIONS

1. After we believe in Jesus Christ in our heart and receive his salvation, we must begin to grow spiritually. List some different ways we refer to this process of spiritual growth.

2. What is a disciple of Christ? A disciple of Christ is:

3. What one thing is our key to spiritual growth?

4. How did the Bible come to us?

5. How does the Holy Spirit help us to understand the Bible?

6. What kind of attitude should we have when we come to read and study the Bible?

7. What two words describe the Bible as food for our spiritual growth?

8. What kind of spiritual food from question 7 above do you need at this time in your life?

9. List 4 things the Bible is for us to help us grow spiritually.

10. List 5 things we need to do with our Bible to grow spiritually.

11. Do you have a copy of the Bible? If not, please let us know.

3. A PERSONAL MINISTRY FOR GOD

THEME: IN A NUT SHELL

BLOCK 6 - THEME 1 - LESSON 3

LESSON AIM: Show that God wants each one of us to have a personal ministry for him.

There are two statements that we often hear that each touch on the purpose of life but end up leaving us without a clue as to what to do or how to do it. Perhaps you have heard someone say something like this, "God has a wonderful purpose for your life." But, they cannot tell you very much about this purpose and how to find it, or how to fulfill it should you happen to find it. The other statement is just as bleak. They say, "I know God has left me here for a reason; I just don't know what it is."

Beyond this, there are also so many shallow interpretations that people offer for our purpose in life. Some say that the purpose for our life may be simply to open a door for a stranger or offer a smile to those who cross our paths every day. While these are admirable things to do, if they are ends in themselves, they are so far short of the purpose God had in mind when he created us and when he went to the extent of dying on the cross and rising from the dead.

The purpose of God for our lives can be seen in relation to the church (Ephesians 3:20-21). Let's take a look at three points which will help us to see how this is so.

It can be said that Christ has two bodies. The first one is the physical body that he had while he lived on the earth some 2,000 years ago. It is a body just like ours; one that grew physically, experienced fatigue, thirst, hunger, joy, sadness, pain, suffering, and even death (Philippians 2:5-8). Jesus still lives in that body today and in it, he is seated in heaven at the right hand of God, a place of power and authority.

Jesus also has a second body in which he lives today. This is his body, the church (Ephesians 1:19-23). In this body, Jesus lives just like we live in the world. We are an invisible personality living in a visible body. Everything we do in the world, we have to do through our body. God works in the world through his body, the church, in the same way. We are his feet, going to the places and to the peoples who have a need for him in their life. We are his hands, touching those who need a touch from God. We are his voice, bearing the news of his salvation to the lost of the world. He works through us as his body in the world.

God promised a blessing to all the peoples of the world (Genesis 12:1-3). This promise would be found in the person of the Lord Jesus Christ and the salvation that he made possible through his death on the cross and bodily resurrection from the dead. The news of this blessing would be carried to the nations of the world through his people. The Hebrew race had this privilege in the beginning. Through disobedience, they lost this privilege. At this time, the task has been given to his church. The church now has to accomplish this purpose of God on behalf of Christ and for the benefit of the nations (Matthew 28:18-20).

Taking the gospel to the nations obviously can be done in two ways. First, in the United States, the nations have come to us. People from other ethnic groups from all over the world now live in our neighborhoods. We go to the same schools. We shop in the same stores. We work at the same job sites. It is now possible to cross the ethnic boundaries of the nations without leaving our local towns, cities and counties. The nations have literally come to our doorsteps. In this way, God has made it easier for us to engage the nations with the gospel of the Lord Jesus Christ.

Another way to evangelize the nations is still by the old fashioned way; we can continue to go to where they are. To speak of the nations primarily is to speak of ethnic groups, not of geographical boundaries. But geographical boundaries are still part of the equation. When the nations are not within our physical reach, we can go to where they are. In recent years, many Christians have participated in short-term mission trips which have taken them into other countries where they have had the opportunity to take the gospel to the people in their homeland. This is a possibility that must be a part of our strategy of impacting the world with the gospel. We are to take the good news to the nations and make disciples of Christ. This is the practical purpose of the church in the world today.

The purpose of God for our life has to be thought of in two areas. The first area we can call God's general purpose for our life. The Bible tells us in no uncertain terms what God's general purpose is for our life. We do not have to guess at it or try to come up with a purpose on our own. God has called us out from the world that he might send us back into the world with the message of reconciliation through Jesus Christ (Mark 3:14) (John 17:18; 20:21). Those whom he calls out, after a period of spiritual development God sends out to the nations of the world with this good news of redemption and salvation. Upon hearing the gospel of Christ and believing in him, we are all to be engaged in the process of helping these new believers to become disciples, or learners and followers, of Jesus Christ. They too, in time, will do the same with others also (2Timothy 2:2). Christians refer to this purpose with the term, "The Great Commission". This is God's general purpose and it is the same for each and every follower of Christ (Matthew 28:18-20). There are no exclusions or exceptions.

The second area in which we are to think of God's purpose is in terms of his specific purpose for us as an individual. We are all intended to take the good news of salvation to all peoples of the world and to make disciples of the believers. The next thing we will have to determine is the specific way in which each of us will perform this task. God does not simply want us to do something for him; he wants us to do something specific for him (Ephesians 2:10). Therefore, we can say concerning the purpose of God that there is a track to follow, and there is a track to find.

We may think of God's purpose in terms of a railroad track. On one side, the track of God's general purpose has already been laid: he wants us to make disciples in all nations. It is up to us as individuals to lay the parallel track of our specific purpose in the unique way we will fulfill the Great Commission.

While the general purpose is clearly revealed to us in the Bible, the specific purpose for each of us is not. The specific purpose is the way that we as an individual will fulfill the great commission (1Corinthians 12:12-27). This is what we have to find along the way in life. The Bible does give us some clues to help us find this specific purpose. God has chosen the very place each one of us will occupy in the body of

Christ. Another way to state this place is to refer to it as our personal ministry. To help us determine this place he has chosen, God has given us two things.

First, he has placed a desire within our heart that matches the works or ministry he wants us to accomplish in our place of service within the body of Christ (Psalms 37:3-5). It is easy to miss this clue since it is right under our nose. It is a legitimate consideration to think about the things you really like and enjoy doing. This can be a clue to help us discover the way we can take the gospel to the nations in a way in which we would really enjoy doing it. It is possible to make a world-impacting ministry out of almost anything.

Another clue we have is our spiritual gift (Romans 12). When we were saved, God gave us a gift. This gift equips us to do the work that he has planned and for which he has given us a desire to accomplish. There are seven possible categories of spiritual gifts that we might have. And we have at least one of them. It is out of this gift and in conjunction with our heart's desire that we find the place God has designed for us in the body of Christ and consequently, the work, or the specific way in which we can fulfill his general purpose of making disciples in the nations of the world.

Yet another important part of the process of discovering our specific purpose is through an up-close, personal relationship with a more mature Christian (Philippians 1:1). We might call this person a mentor, a coach, or a teacher. A more Biblical title might be something like disciple-maker. Every Christian needs such a one in their life. We need this relationship to see a model of what we are to become and to help us grow. There is nothing that will be more beneficial to you in your maturing process and there is no substitute for it. It will make all the difference in the world in the progress you make along the way.

All of these clues (desire, spiritual gift, discipling relationship) have to be supported with your own personal study of the Bible and prayer. The Bible is the basis of all the ways God will speak to you. Prayer is how you will speak to him. Bible study and prayer are the means through which we commune, or fellowship with God (Ephesians 6:13-18). Through these, God will reveal his purpose for our life.

We are a part of Christ's church in the world. He wants us to take his good news to all peoples, making disciples of them for his sake. Each Christian has a key role to play in this effort. To fulfill our role, we must know God's general purpose and his specific purpose for our life.

These important discoveries do not fall upon us out of the sky. We will have to search for them. We will have to follow the clues we are given. We will have to journey to find them. It may be difficult. It may take a long time. But we can make the discovery. And, it will be worth it when we do. Let's ask God to help us find our way.

"Heavenly Father. Thank you for making a special place in your church just for me. Thank you for showing us through the Bible, your general purpose of making disciples in all nations. Help me to find the specific way you would have me to fulfill this purpose. When I find it, help me to arrange my life around your purpose for as long as I may live. Help me to live my life for this greater cause and purpose. In Jesus name I pray. Amen."

A PERSONAL MINISTRY FOR GOD
BLOCK 6 - THEME 1 - LESSON 3 (183 OF 216)
LESSON OUTLINE

I THE CHURCH IS THE BODY OF CHRIST IN THE WORLD TODAY
A. Christ's physical body
B. Christ's mystical body

II GOD'S PURPOSE FOR THE CHURCH IS TO TAKE HIS GOSPEL TO THE NATIONS
A. The nations have come to us
B. We can go to the nations

III AS A PART OF THE CHURCH, YOU HAVE A PURPOSE TO FULFILL
A. God's general purpose for your life
B. God's specific purpose for your life (clues to finding)
  1. The desire of our heart
  2. Our spiritual gift
  3. A discipling relationship
  4. Personal Bible study and prayer

SCRIPTURES TO BROADEN YOUR UNDERSTANDING
1. God's purpose for your life
   Matthew 28:18-20
   Acts 1:8
   1 Thessalonians 1:4

2. Jesus seated in heaven
   Colossians 3:1

3. God works through us
   2 Corinthians 5:20

4. God turns from the Jews to the church
   Romans 9-11

LINES OF THEOLOGICAL CONNECTION
1. ECCLESIOLOGY
   Preaching the gospel of Jesus Christ
   World Missions
   Disciple-making

2. CHRISTOLOGY
   Jesus lives in the believer

3. ANTHROPOLOGY
   The desire of the heart
   Spiritual gifts
   Personal relationship with God

LESSON GLOSSARY

1. Reconciliation
   To bring together

2. Mentor
   A personal guide

A PERSONAL MINISTRY FOR GOD
BLOCK 6 - THEME 1 - LESSON 3 (183 OF 216)
QUESTIONS

1. What is the best way to begin to understand God's purpose for your life?

2. List the two bodies of Christ in the world.

3. What is God's purpose for the church?

4. What are the two areas in which we can think of the purpose of God?

5. What is another phrase for God's general purpose?

6. List two ways to take the gospel to the nations.

7. What are we referring to by the phrase, the specific purpose of God?

8. List four clues that will help you discover God's specific purpose for your life.

9. Have you discovered God's specific purpose for your life? If so, what is it?

10. What kind of ministry would you like to be involved in?

4. EVANGELISM

THEME: IN A NUT SHELL

BLOCK 6 - THEME 1 - LESSON 4

LESSON AIM: Show that God wants each one of us to share the good news of salvation through Jesus Christ with others.

SCRIPTURE: (1 John 1:4)

"We want you to be with us in this - in this fellowship with the Father, and Jesus Christ his Son. We must write and tell you about it, because the more that fellowship extends, the greater the joy it brings to us who are already in it." (1John 1:4) Phillips

It is a wonderful experience to grow in Christ. It is great to understand that the church can tell me how to have a right relationship with God, how to become more than I am now, and how to live for a greater purpose. The only thing as good as all of these is when we can help another person to make these discoveries also. This is another reason the church should be important to me; it helps me increase the value of my life for God by helping others to learn these same things.

When we read the line above, we might protest. After all, God is infinite, isn't he? If he is infinite, is it possible that we can add to or take away from his value in the world, and if we can, how can we do it? The answer is, yes we can. It is possible for us to add to the value of God in the world (John 17:4). And, since it is possible to add to his value, it is also possible to take away from his value in the world.

Consider how we can decrease the value of God in the world. Let's use two digits for a simple illustration; the numbers 0 and 1. Let the zero represent us since in ourselves and apart from Christ we are nothing. Let the 1 represent Jesus since he is whole and is to be first in all things. If I, as a zero place myself in front of the number 1, I decrease the value of the 1 by 100 times [.01]. If I influence another person to follow me in my own preeminence, we decrease the value of the 1 by 1,000 times [.001]. You can easily see how by influencing others in a negative way, we can bring discredit and decrease to the value of God through our life.

On the other hand, if we align our self properly in relation to Christ, we can increase his value in the world. A 0 on the right side of the 1 increases its value by 10 times [10]. Get another 0 and we increase its value by 100 times [100]. In the same way, we can increase the value of God in the world by proper alignment in relation to Jesus.

Just as you can increase the value of God in the world, you can increase the value of your own life by inviting others to follow you as you follow Christ. You do this first of all by giving them an example to follow (2Timothy 3:10-11). You model before them what it is to be a Christian. You open your life in such a way that you let them see how you interact with God. You let them see your struggles, your questions, your wrestling over the issues. You also let them see your faith in God and his Word. You show them how you pray and believe God for the things you commit to him. You let them see your confidence and hope in the Lord. You show them how to read and study the Bible and how to pray. You let them watch you and work with you as you work in the lives of others in all kinds of situations. In doing so, by the influence of your own life you press into them the image of Christ himself. Before long, they begin to understand that they can live in the same way. After a while, you will have found another zero that you can line up with yourself beside Christ, increasing both his value and yours in the world.

While you model the Christian life before them, you also teach them all that you know about Christ and his way of life (Colossians 1:28-29). You get them involved in the Scriptures, reading them and studying them. You show them how to connect the dots between the stories of the people in the Bible with Christ himself. You teach them to rely upon the Holy Spirit as they study the Word. You show them how to use tools for Bible study. You call upon them to look deeper and to see more from the text. You help them to see the relevance and to make personal application of the ancient Scriptures in their life today. You feed them the milk of the Word until it becomes the meat of the Word.

Next, you give them little pieces of the work to do themselves (Luke 10). They can try out the things they have learned while you are there to guide them along. If they make a mistake, you are there to correct them. If they miss the point of it all, you can call their attention to this and steer them in the right way. If they make a total flop, you can pick them up, dust them off, and give them another opportunity to try it again. Pretty soon, they will have it and will be able to do the work without your direct supervision.

Finally, when you have brought them far enough along, you turn them loose to do the same thing with others, requiring them to do the same thing with others. Through this multiplying effort, spiritual reproduction takes place. Continual reproduction is insured into the future. Paul told Timothy, "What you have heard of me in the presence of many witnesses, the same commit thou to faithful men who shall be able to teach others also" (Timothy 2:2). Through the multiplication of other disciples of Christ, you increase the value of God in the world, you increase your own value in the world, you fulfill the Lord's Great Commission, you help other people to have true joy in their life, and you bring joy to yourself and to other Christians. These are among the endless benefits of investing your life into other people with a goal of spiritual reproduction. This is how you can increase the value of your own life for God.

You are a fortunate individual if you have a church in your community that is working to help you know and understand why the church should be important to you in your life. The church is important because it tells you how to have a right relationship with God, it tells you how to become much more than you are now, it tells you how to live your life for a greater purpose, and it tells you how to increase the value of your life for God by helping others to make these same discoveries. Your life can count in a significant way for the glory of God. You can make your mark in the world by being a part of this church in your community. Together we can become more and accomplish more in the world for God's glory. We encourage you to find a church in your community where you can join in the work God is doing in the world. Pray this prayer from your heart to God.

"Our Father. Thank you that I can increase the value of your life and mine in the world through reproducing more followers of Christ. Help me to learn this process and to live it in all of my relationships with other people. Please lead me to a church where I can learn, grow, and serve. In Jesus name I pray. Amen."

EVANGELISM
BLOCK 6 - THEME 1- LESSON 4 (184 OF 216)
LESSON OUTLINE

I YOU CAN INCREASE GOD'S VALUE IN THE WORLD
   A. Decreasing God's value - Putting ourself before God
   B. Increasing God's value - Putting God first

II YOU CAN INCREASE YOUR VALUE IN THE WORLD
   A. Be a model others can follow
   B. Teach others to follow Christ
   C. Assign work and check behind them
   D. Require them to reproduce other Christ followers

SCRIPTURES TO BROADEN YOUR UNDERSTANDING
1. Bringing God glory
   John 17:4

2. Multiplying your life
   2 Timothy 2:2

LINES OF THEOLOGICAL CONNECTION
1. DISCIPLE-MAKING
   Modeling
   Multiplication

2. EVANGELISM
   Soul-winning
   Sharing the gospel

Allen L. Elder

EVANGELISM
BLOCK 6 - THEME 1- LESSON 4 (184 OF 216)
QUESTIONS

1. We all at times have done things to decrease God's value in the world. Are you seeking now to increase God's value in the world, and if so, how?

2. Can you name a person who has had a spiritual influence in your life?

3. Who do you know that would be willing to have you make a spiritual investment into their life?

4. What will you do to make an effort to make that investment into their life?

22

5. A CHRISTIAN IS A CHILD OF GOD

THEME: TRUTHS ABOUT CHRISTIANS

BLOCK 6 - THEME 2 - LESSON 1

LESSON AIM: Show that God considers those who believe in Christ as his children.

SCRIPTURE: (John 1:12)

But as many as received him, to them gave he power to become the sons of God, even to them that believe on his name:

Every person born into the world still feels the effects of Adam's sin from Genesis chapter three. We feel those effects in our lives on the outside and on the inside. We live in a world that does not seek after God. The world's system pulls at us so that we might remain in a state of separation from God. It seeks to conform us to its own mold, drawing us away, keeping us bound in the slavery of sin. This bondage has many forms. For some people, it requires the lowest depths of man's depravity to keep them away from God. These are those people who commit some of the most heinous acts of humanity. But for most people, the allure of the world does not have to be to that degree. Many people are just content with a nice house and other belongings, a good job and retirement, and to be left alone without the responsibilities of being a follower of Christ in the world. Either way, in this example, one person is just as bound by the world as the other. These are some of the outward effects of sin.

We also feel the inward effects of sin. From the very beginning of our life, our adversary, the devil and his messengers are waged in a spiritual war against us. They know the great potential of a person's life that grows in Christ, learns what God wants to do with their life, and seeks to fulfil the purpose of God every day. The enemy starts very early to derail God's purpose from taking place in our life. They expose us to all manner of sin and spiritually unhealthy conditions in an attempt to keep us from knowing the good things God has in store for those who trust in him. They work to trap us in the life-long practice of sin. They chip away at our self-worth and dignity, seeking to make us feel worthless and unwanted. Any bad thing imaginable is in the devil's arsenal to steal, kill, and destroy the life, testimony, and influence of a Christian. We feel these inward effects of sin as well.

Part of the wonder of being a Christian is to begin to realize all that God has done for us in salvation through Jesus Christ. There are so many wonderful things he has in store both in this life and in eternity beyond this life. In fact, those things are so many and wonderful that the Bible says that we have never seen, heard, or even thought of the things God has in store for those who belong to him. There are some things, however, that we can begin to get our minds around and enjoy right now. One of these things is the fact that those who believe in Christ are the children of God.

This is such wonderful news considering the damage the devil can do in our lives before, and even after, we believe in Christ. To become the child of God is like having been an abused child, growing up in a filthy and vile environment with the meanest father imaginable and being adopted into the best family in town with the dearest dad in the neighborhood. In reality, it is even much better than this. If you have believed on Jesus Christ in your heart, one of the first things you need to really get into your mind is the fact that you are a child of God. You have a new spiritual father and a new family. As a believer, you have come home.

Let's consider four things about being a child of God from the Bible. First, as a child of God, you have been born into God's family. The physical birth into the world does not make us a child of God. To become a child of God requires a spiritual new birth, or a second birth. This birth takes place deep within us in our spirit through the work of the Holy Spirit and through our belief of the truth about Jesus. Jesus said this to a man named Nicodemus, and it is true for every person in the history of the world, "You must be born again." The new birth, or regeneration as it is called in theological terms, happens as we believe.

Second, to be born again means that we are a brand new baby in the family of God. As it is in the physical life, new babies have to grow and learn. They have to learn to crawl, walk, talk, work, and every other thing that has to be done. The Christian life is a growing process. It is a sad condition when a person has been a Christian for many years but has failed to grow and remains as it were, a babe in Christ. God wants us to grow and mature because he has work for us to do. He wants to give us responsibility for his work. He cannot entrust his important things to baby Christians. This would be like giving the car keys to a toddler and putting him behind the wheel of a moving vehicle. It would be a catastrophe. We must mature so we can take part in the work God is doing.

To be a child of God also means that all of our old family ties with our old father, the devil, have been broken. We no longer have to do the things he wants us to do. Those things are sin. God has made it possible, now that we are in the family of God, for us to be free from sin. We no longer have to give ourselves in service to sin. We can choose to give ourselves to the service of God, who is our new Father in faith. This, or course, is not an easy thing to do. It will be a continual struggle for us for the rest of our lives. Sometimes we will do well and be able to resist the draw and temptation of sin. Other times, we will give in in spite of our desire not to sin. Although we are saved, we still live in these bodies of flesh and the flesh does not want spiritual things. The spirit and the flesh are at war with each other and this war takes place within our bodies. We have to learn to be good soldiers, fighting the good fight of faith, to win over this great struggle. It can be done. The Bible tells us how to have victories in this warfare. We have to fight, and it is not always easy. But we can win through the Christ who lives within us.

The last thing to note in this lesson about being a child of God is that we have access to our father. There is a famous picture from the Oval Office of President Kennedy's son, John Jr., playing under the desk of his father, the President of the United States of America. This is a good illustration of the access we have to our father who is the only true and living God of the whole world. Through the death of Jesus on the cross, we have been given access to the throne of God, and to the God who sits on this throne. We can come boldly to him, the Bible says, that we may get the mercy and grace we need in the time of need. God wants us to come to him with our needs, but we also have access to him whenever we just want to crawl up in his lap and let him love on us and sing to us and let us love him back. This fact is brought out in the Bible when it refers to God in his deepest relational form as a daddy. God is our God, our Father, and our daddy. He wants us to know him in this intimate way.

It is a wonderful thing to be a child of God. This is a relationship which can never be broken. Absolutely nothing in the universe can separate us from the love of God which is in Christ Jesus. Do you know the father in this way today? Have you believed on Jesus Christ? Are you a child of God? You can be. Call on him and believe. He will give you the power to become a son of God.

A CHRISTIAN IS A CHILD OF GOD
BLOCK 6 - THEME 2 - LESSON 1 (185 OF 216)
LESSON OUTLINE

Four truths about being a child of God

I WE HAVE A NEW BIRTH
    A. Regeneration
    B. Belief of the truth

II WE MUST GROW IN CHRIST
    A. The Christian life is a growing process
    B. We must grow to be trusted with responsibility

III OLD FAMILY TIES WITH THE DEVIL HAVE BEEN BROKEN
    A. The devil was our spiritual father
    B. God is now our Father

IV WE HAVE ACCESS TO OUR FATHER IN HEAVEN
    A. For fellowship
    B. For help

SCRIPTURES TO BROADEN YOUR UNDERSTANDING
1. Love not the world
    1 John 2:15-16

2. Do not be conformed to the world
    Romans 12:1-2

3. We serve whom we obey
    Romans 6:16

4. The devil has come to destroy
   John 10:10

5. God has prepared wonderful things for his people
   1 Corinthians 2:9

6. An example of the devil's destructive power
   Job 1-2

7. We are the sons of God
   Romans 8:1-17

8. The new birth
   John 3:1-21

9. Grow in Christ
   2 Peter 3:18
   2 Timothy 2:15

10. Salvation
    2 Thessalonians 2:13
    Ephesians 2:8-9

11. The old father, the devil
    John 8:44

12. Winning through Christ
    Philippians 4:13

13. Access to God
    Hebrews 5:16

14. Nothing can break our relationship with God
    Romans 8:33-39

15. Trusting God
    Romans 10:9-10
    Acts 16:30-31

16. Assurance of salvation
    1 John 5:13

LINES OF THEOLOGICAL CONNECTION
1. SOTERIOLOGY
   God's choosing
   Faith
   Regeneration
   Eternal security
   Assurance of salvation

2. THE DOCTRINE OF SATAN
   Father of lies and all evil

3. DOCTRINE OF SIN
   The fall
   Living apart from sin

4. ANTHROPOLOGY
   Spiritual growth
   Sharing in God's work

LESSON GLOSSARY
1. Regeneration
   The work of the Holy Spirit to bring about our new birth in Christ

2. Access
   To get to; approach

A CHRISTIAN IS A CHILD OF GOD
BLOCK 6 - THEME 2 - LESSON 1 (185 OF 216)
QUESTIONS

1. Where do we feel the effects of sin?

2. What are some examples of the inward effects of sin?

3. What inward or outward effects of sin might you be dealing with today?

4. As you read Job 1-2, what is your reaction to the destructive power of the devil in a person's life?

5. List the four facts mentioned in this lesson about being a child of God.

6. Are you growing in Christ as a child of God? Give some evidence of your growth.

6. A CHRISTIAN IS A NEW CREATION IN CHRIST

THEME: TRUTHS ABOUT CHRISTIANS

BLOCK 6 - THEME 2 - LESSON 2

LESSON AIM: Show that Christians are new creations in Christ and should live for God's purpose.

SCRIPTURE: (2 Corinthians 5:17; Ephesians 4:17-24; Colossians 2:11)

Therefore if any man be in Christ, he is a new creature: old things are passed away; behold, all things are become new.

To become a Christian is to have a brand new start in life. This is such good news. For many of us, life, even at a young age, can already be in such a mess. Our relationship with God gives us a new beginning. This does not mean that our immediate situation necessarily changes, but it does mean that we have been changed. And when we have been changed, we can begin to work ourselves out of whatever bad environment into which life may have landed us.

2 Corinthians 5:17 gives us three points to consider in this new condition of being in Christ. First, we are a new creation. We live in the same body. The same face looks back at us when we look into the mirror. Yet, on the inside, in the deepest, truest part of us - in our heart - we are a brand new creation. Through the blood of Jesus Christ, God has removed our sin from his sight. In Christ, God looks at us as if we have never sinned at all. The Bible calls this portion of salvation justification. Justification means to declare righteous. The righteousness of Christ has been applied to our spirit and we are new in him. In the sight of God, we are now righteous.

As it was stated above, salvation does not necessarily change our physical situation or environment. We still have to live in the world and among other people who may not know Christ. As a Christian, we now have to learn to not allow ourselves to be led away from God by others. When they invite us to participate in ungodly things, we have to fight off the temptation to do things that are not pleasing to God. This is the second thing Paul speaks of in our verse of study. He said that the old has passed away. The old man, as the Bible calls the flesh, has died in Christ. However, the continuing battle for the Christian is to not allow the devil to get us to live in the flesh anymore.

Paul expounded on this idea in several other passages of Scripture: Romans chapters 6 through 8; Galatians 5:16-26; Ephesians 4:17-24; and Colossians 2:11 and

3:8-9. Take the time to read all of this Scripture to get an understanding of what it is to battle the temptation of the flesh. Now that you are a new creature in Christ, there is a war going on within you. It is a war between the old man, or the old way of life before knowing Christ, and the new man, the new person you are now that you are saved. It is a war over how you will choose to live your life as a Christian. You can give in to the flesh and be disobedient to God, or you can surrender to the Spirit and accomplish the things God has planned for you to do. This war will continue as long as you live on the earth. The more you learn about it and practice your surrender to the Spirit, the more the enemy will come after you with even greater temptation. But, at the same time, thc more you will become stronger in Christ and the more you will accomplish for Christ.

Paul talked about this warfare in terms of putting off the old man and putting on the new man. This will be your daily struggle as a believer in Jesus Christ. There will be days when you will win the battle over the flesh. You will yield to the Spirit of God and you will do the things God wants you to do. There will be other times when, in spite of your greatest desire not to give in to the flesh, you will do it anyway and sin. You are not the only one who has this experience. Every believer in Christ has done this, even the great men of the Bible. You can read about Paul's struggle with this very thing in Romans chapter 7. The thing you must do when this happens is to admit your sin to God, ask his cleansing and forgiveness, and turn away from it. If you let yourself continue in sin and try to live under the guilt of it, you will be defeated as a Christian. There is even now no condemnation to those who are in Christ Jesus. Do not let the enemy cause you to carry the guilt of your sin. This is why we confess it and repent of it. God does not want us to wallow in it, but to rebound from it to live as the new creation we are in him.

The third thing Paul says in 2 Corinthians 5:17 is that all things are now new for the believer in Christ. In Christ, God has opened the door to everything that he wants his children to experience with him. This certainly considers all that God has planned and is preparing for us to enjoy and do throughout eternity. But it also includes all the wonderful things God has in store for his people right now on the earth. God is at work calling out the church from among all people groups on earth. He calls us to be a part of this work with him. Long before God created the world, he planned works that he would use you to accomplish in relation to this work. Ephesians 2:10 directly links our new creation in Christ to the works he has planned for us to do. Can you imagine this? Even before God created the world, he was thinking of you and of the work you would do with him. We can relate to this when we think about that person that we love and want to spend the rest of our life with. We daydream about all the wonderful things we will enjoy in the future when our lives are finally brought together in matrimony. God had thoughts like this too, looking ahead into the future to us and to the work we would do with him. Can you feel the love from his heart toward you right now as you think on these things?

God has work he wants us to do for him. This is one of the reasons he went to the extent of rescuing us from the fall and recreating us in Christ. He did this not just so we could be a good person and try not to sin. He did it so he could accomplish the work he wants to do through us. The thing we have to do after we are saved is to try to figure out what it is that God wants us to do and how he wants us to do it. We all are to work for the same goal but we will all do it in different ways. This different way is what we have to find.

What about you? Have you started to think about what God wants you to do for him with your life? We go to a lot of trouble to decide on a career path for our life. We go to school and get degrees in certain fields of study. Then, we get jobs and work and make money to support ourselves and our families. It is possible to do all of this and to have a good life from the world's point of view and to completely miss that one thing that God wants you to be and do.

God saved us. He bought us with the price of the blood of his Son, Jesus. He has made it possible for us to no longer live after the flesh. He has made us a brand new creation in him. The least we can do is to give our life to him and for him that his plans for us in this world might come to pass.

A CHRISTIAN IS A NEW CREATION IN CHRIST
BLOCK 6 - THEME 2 - LESSON 2 (186 OF 216)
LESSON OUTLINE

Three points to consider about being in Christ

I WE ARE A NEW CREATION IN CHRIST
A. We are the same outwardly
B. We are new inwardly

II THE OLD MAN IS PASSED AWAY
A. The old man is dead
B. We are now in a warfare between the old man and the new man

III ALL THINGS ARE NEW IN CHRIST
A. God has wonderful things for us in eternity
B. God has wonderful things for us on earth

SCRIPTURES TO BROADEN YOUR UNDERSTANDING
1. God has justified us
   Romans 5:1-2

2. God has removed our sin from his sight
   Colossians 2:14-15
   Isaiah 44:22-23

3. We still struggle with sin
   Romans 1-8

4. We are in the world but not of the world
   John 17:11-18

5. The old man is dead
   Romans 6:6-16

6. Living in Christ and Christ living in us
   Galatians 2:20

7. God has planned work for us
   Ephesians 2:10

8. We should commit our lives to the Lord
   Romans 12:1-2

LINES OF THEOLOGICAL CONNECTION
1. SOTERIOLOGY
   Justification

2. ANTHROPOLOGY
   Spiritual warfare

3. THE DOCTRINE OF SIN
   How to deal with sin

LESSON GLOSSARY
1. Justification
   To declare righteous

A CHRISTIAN IS A NEW CREATION IN CHRIST
BLOCK 6 - THEME 2 - LESSON 2 (186 OF 216)
QUESTIONS

1. What does it mean to us to know God and to become a Christian?

2. Have you believed on Jesus in your heart in order to have this new beginning?

3. The Scripture tells us that we do not have to be a slave to sin. What does this news do for you?

4. God wants us to have friends who do not know him so we can share the gospel with them. Among your lost friends, who has more influence in the other one's life; you or them?

5. What are some ways you experience the struggle between the old man and the new man?

6. What should you do when you sin?

7. How are you working with God in his work right now?

8. Do you have any plans for your future work with God?

7. A CHRISTIAN HAS NO CONDEMNATION

THEME: TRUTHS ABOUT CHRISTIANS

BLOCK 6 - THEME 2 - LESSON 3

LESSON AIM: Show that God has removed his condemnation from those who believe in Christ.

SCRIPTURE: (Romans 5:12-19; 8:1; 33-39)

There is therefore now no condemnation to them which are in Christ Jesus, who walk not after the flesh, but after the Spirit.

In our judicial system in the United States, when a person is convicted of a crime, he bears the consequences of his actions. We refer to these consequences with words like guilty, judgment, sentence, and condemnation. When the perpetrator is found guilty, he is sentenced to pay the consequences of his crime and is said to be under condemnation of the law of the land and the judicial system. In order to be relieved of this condemnation, he has to pay the price for his crime. He either has to complete his sentence or be pardoned. When man sinned against God in the Garden of Eden, God pronounced him guilty and sentenced him to death. Now, all people born into the world enter life bearing the guilt of sin and are under the condemnation of God. We all will either bear the sentence of eternal death and separation from God or we can be pardoned.

Sin came into the world through one man, Adam. When Adam sinned, he still contained the seed of the human race within himself. As God looks at it, in Adam, we all sinned against him. The Bible says in Roman 5:12, by one man sin entered into the world and death by sin. That sin was passed along to everyman, so, in God's sight, all people have sinned and bear his condemnation. We have to take this very personally. In Adam, we sinned too. And, we stand guilty before God. If this condition is not changed at some point in our lifetime upon the earth, we will suffer the eternal consequences of our sin. We will spend eternity in a place called hell which burns with fire and brimstone, being tormented and forsaken by God forever with no possibility of escape or pardon.

The good news is there is a way out from under God's condemnation and to avoid the eternal sentence and consignment to hell. Jesus Christ made the way out through his death on the cross. He came to the earth and actually took our place, bore our sins upon himself along with their guilt, and paid the price with his own sinless life. God has accepted the death of Christ in exchange for our sin. Jesus is the propitiation for the sins of all the peoples of the world. He is the one and only way out of condemnation before God. The Bible says if we will believe on him in our heart, and confess him with our mouth, we will be saved.

When we believe in Christ, something wonderful happens not only within us but also in the sight of God. We become a new creature in Christ, and our standing is changed in the eyes of God. We who were under condemnation by the offense of Adam are now pronounced not guilty before God. In the same way that Adam's sin was charged to our account, the righteousness of Christ is charged to our account when we believe. This act of the imputation of the righteousness of Christ to us is called justification in the Bible. Justification means to declare righteous. This is our new standing before God. We are no longer under his condemnation. The penalty for our sin has been removed because Jesus paid that penalty for us on the cross. The debt has been paid, and we are declared as righteous as Jesus is in the eyes of God. God covers our sin with the blood of Christ and he forgets it. Now, God looks at us as if we never sinned at all. This standing is a reality for those who believe in Christ.

Our adversary, the devil, does not want us to know this truth. He does not want us to know that our debt has been paid in Christ. He does not want us to know that we do not have to bear the guilt of our sin. If he can keep this information hidden from us, or if he can cause us to misunderstand it or refuse to believe it, he can keep us defeated, and we will not reach our potential as a servant of God. We can have victory over Satan by believing the Bible when it says we are no longer guilty. The debt for our sin has been paid in Christ. We are no longer under condemnation.

Having God's condemnation removed from our life is a reality. It happens when we believe on Christ and acknowledge his death on the cross as payment for our sin. There are three things we need to note about this removal of condemnation. First it is immediate. The instant we believe, the condemnation is removed. We are justified in Christ. In the sin of Adam, man experienced spiritual death. Justification is salvation of the spirit. In Christ, our spirit has been raised to life again. God declares us righteous. This is an immediate exchange which happens as we believe in Christ.

We can also say that the removal of condemnation is a present reality. Romans 8:1 says there is *now* no condemnation to those who are in Christ Jesus. This is not something we have to wait to experience when we finally get to heaven, but it is a reality we can enjoy right now. As it was stated above, we no longer have to bear the guilt of our sin. We can forget about it as God has. This brings peace and rest to our hearts when we realize there is no longer a reason to feel guilty before God. Guilt is a weapon of the enemy by which he can hinder or prevent our work for the Lord. Justification defeats this weapon of our adversary.

Third, we must recognize that having no condemnation before God is an eternal reality. This is a condition which can never change. There will never come a time when God will say we are no longer righteous in his sight. Since our righteousness is based on the righteousness of Christ, to lose it would mean that Jesus would have to lose his righteousness, and this is not possible. He is the Lord, he does not change. It is not possible for him to sin. He will ever be as he is now; pure and holy and without sin. Our righteousness is eternal because the righteousness of Christ is eternal. In the end of Romans chapter 8, Paul reminds us that there is absolutely nothing in this world, above the world, or under the world which can ever separate us from the love of God which is in Christ. Our relationship with him is eternal. Our justification is eternal. The removal of condemnation from our life is eternal. We live in the eternal *now* and there is no condemnation to those who are in Christ Jesus.

This truth should encourage us to go forward for the Lord in our work for him. It gives us the upper hand over the enemy who wants us to keep feeling guilty over our sin. It reminds us that we are forever in a new standing before God which can never change. It shows us some of the wonderful things God has done for us in Christ. It would be a tragedy for you to hear of these blessings but never experience them. These blessing can be yours if you will believe on Jesus in your heart. Do this now if you have not done so. If you have believed in Christ, then also believe the Bible when it says you are no longer condemned in the eyes of God. You stand before him in the righteousness of Christ. Go in that righteousness and accomplish the things God has planned for your life.

A CHRISTIAN HAS NO CONDEMNATION
BLOCK 6 - THEME 2 - LESSON 3 (187 OF 216)
LESSON OUTLINE

In Christ, God's condemnation is removed from the believer.

I IMMEDIATE REMOVAL
A. God's condemnation is removed when we believe in Christ
B. We are pronounced not guilty by God

II A PRESENT REALITY
A. There is NOW no condemnation in Christ
B. This brings peace to our heart

III AN ETERNAL REALITY
A. Our righteousness is in Christ
B. Christ will never change

SCRIPTURES TO BROADEN YOUR UNDERSTANDING
1. The price of sin is death
   Romans 6:23

2. We are all guilty of sin against God
   Romans 3:23

3. Jesus paid the price for our sins
   Romans 5:6

4. Jesus is the only way of salvation
   John 14:6
   Acts 4:12

5. Jesus' death satisfies God for our sin
   1 John 2:2

6. Jesus paid the sin debt in full
   John 19:30

LINES OF THEOLOGICAL CONNECTION
1. THE DOCTRINE OF SIN
   Imputed sin
   Imparted sin
   Personal sin
   Guilt of sin

2. CHRISTOLOGY
   Jesus is the redeemer

LESSON GLOSSARY
1. Condemnation
   To be in a state of guilt and deserving of punishment

2. Imputation
   To charge or to credit to

A CHRISTIAN HAS NO CONDEMNATION
BLOCK 6 - THEME 2 - LESSON 3 (187 OF 216)
QUESTIONS

1. What does it mean to be under God's condemnation?

2. What is the punishment related to God's condemnation?

3. How does one escape God's condemnation?

4. Why does the devil want to use guilt against you?

5. What is our standing before God based upon?

6. To be pronounced not guilty by God makes us free to work for him. What work are you doing for God with your life?

8. A CHRISTIAN IS ETERNALLY SECURE

THEME: TRUTHS ABOUT CHRISTIANS

BLOCK 6 - THEME 2 - LESSON 4

LESSON AIM: Show that a Christian can never, under any circumstances, lose his salvation in Christ.

SCRIPTURE: (Romans 8:33-39)

38 For I am persuaded, that neither death, nor life, nor angels, nor principalities, nor powers, nor things present, nor things to come, 39 Nor height, nor depth, nor any other creature, shall be able to separate us from the love of God, which is in Christ Jesus our Lord.

Once a person is saved, can he or she ever become unsaved? In other words, can a person lose their salvation in Christ? This is an issue that Christians have wrangled over for centuries. And, as you might guess, some of them answer the question with a "yes", and some of them answer the question with a "no". The correct answer comes from the Bible, and the answer is "no, a Christian cannot lose his salvation in Christ Jesus." Let's consider why this is so.

One of the first observations we must make is that salvation is a much deeper subject than the human mind, apart from the help of the Holy Spirit, can understand on its own in its fullest sense. The issue of salvation goes beyond human understanding and human reasoning. We cannot get to the truth about salvation within ourselves. We must have the help of God's Word and the help of the Holy Spirit to come to some understanding of this subject. The Bible tells us that we cannot even recognize Jesus as Lord without the help of the Holy Spirit. Since this is so, we have to go to God's Word and depend upon him to help us understand this deep and wonderful subject of salvation in Jesus Christ.

In the first place, the Bible uses the term "eternal salvation" to speak of our new birth into the family of God. This makes it pretty simple: salvation is eternal. Since this fact is now established with Scripture, we now have to begin the search to find out the reasons why this is so.

To get a grasp on the subject of salvation, we have to look at it from two perspectives. The first perspective is the human perspective. From our point of view, we heard the gospel and put our faith in Christ through belief of the truth and we were saved. But, there is also the divine perspective. The divine perspective takes us back into the mind and heart of God even before the foundation of the world. It is from this perspective that we begin to realize the eternal aspect of our salvation.

When we begin to look at the deeper issues involved in our salvation, we find that there are basically two reasons why our salvation is eternal and therefore impossible to be lost. The first reason salvation is eternal is because it was purchased with an eternal redemption. When Jesus died on the cross for the sins of the world, he died once, for all, forever. There will never be another need for additional payment for sin. The sacrifice of Christ, one time, was enough for all, and for all time. This is why as he died, he cried out, "Paid in full!" The eternal requirement and payment had been made, and God was satisfied with it. Jesus is the propitiation, or the atonement, for our sins and for the sins of all the peoples of the world. Through Jesus, it is possible for people from every tribe and tongue and kindred on earth to come to God for eternal salvation through him. He made the eternal redemptive payment which God required. Our salvation in Christ is eternal because of the eternal price that Jesus paid for it on the cross.

The second reason our salvation is eternal is that the redemptive price that was paid for it was made by the eternal God himself. This means that our salvation is anchored in the unmovable, unchanging, eternal God of everything. Eternal salvation is anchored in eternal redemption, and eternal redemption was made by the eternal God. Therefore, salvation is eternal because the God who provides it is eternal.

This is one of the reasons why we have to look at the divine perspective as well as the human perspective on salvation. From the human perspective, we know that we heard and believed and confessed our sins and asked Jesus into our hearts. But there are times when we wonder if we said the right things, or if we prayed the right prayer, or if we covered all the bases to make sure that we are saved. In other words, there can be times in our lives when we are not really sure if we are saved at all. We may doubt that we have salvation, or we may not feel like we are saved. These are the times when we have to look beyond our experience of salvation to the fact that our salvation is in God. Since it is in God, it is eternal and can never be lost, regardless of how we may feel.

Another part of eternal salvation with which Christians differ has to do with more information the Bible gives us from the divine perspective. We find many times in the Scriptures a statement made which says that God chose us before we chose him. We are told that God chose us in him before we were born. The Scripture says that God even chose us before he made the world itself. Christians have debated these statements and have even been divided upon them as to what they actually mean. While we may never fully understand these statements, or come to an agreement on what they mean, since they are written in the Word of God we must admit that they do mean something from God's point of view, therefore they have importance to us. We cannot discount them, or deny them, or say they do not mean what they say. We may not understand them, but they add to the solid foundation upon which our salvation in Christ is based. We should carefully and reverently read and study these passages and ask the Holy Spirit to help us understand them. To have some measure of a grasp on them adds to the assurance in our hearts that we do, in fact, possess an eternal salvation.

Those people who have believed in the Lord Jesus Christ in their heart and who have confessed him with their mouth as Savior and Lord have eternal salvation. Salvation is eternal because it was paid for with an eternal redemption. Eternal redemption was made by the eternal God. Therefore, the salvation of the believer is found to be anchored in the eternal God himself. Jesus said in John 10:27-30, "My sheep hear my voice, and I know them, and they follow me: And I give unto them eternal life; and they shall never perish, neither shall any man pluck them out of my hand. My Father, which gave them me, is greater than all; and no man is able to pluck them out of my Father's hand. I and my Father are one."

Be sure that you have entrusted the salvation of your eternal soul to Christ. If you have believed on him in your heart, be assured that the Bible confirms that you are now in a relationship with God which can never be severed. You have an eternal salvation.

A CHRISTIAN IS ETERNALLY SECURE
BLOCK 6 - THEME 2 - LESSON 4 (188 OF 216)
LESSON OUTLINE

Salvation is eternal because

I SALVATION IS FOUNDED IN THE ETERNAL GOD
A. God is eternal
B. God will never change

II ETERNAL REDEMPTION WAS MADE BY THE ETERNAL GOD
A. Jesus paid the price for sin in full
B. No further payment for sin will ever need to be made

III SALVATION IS ETERNAL
A. Salvation is founded in the eternal God
B. Since God is eternal, and redemption is eternal, salvation is eternal

SCRIPTURES TO BROADEN YOUR UNDERSTANDING
1. Redemption is eternal
   Hebrews 9:12

2. Salvation is eternal
   Hebrews 5:9

3. We are chosen in Christ from before the foundation of the world
   John 1:12-13
   John 15:16
   Ephesians 1:3-12
   Ephesians 2
   Romans 8:28-30
   2 Thessalonians 2:13
   2 Timothy 1:9
   1 Peter 1:2; 2:9

4. The Holy Spirit illuminates us
   1 Corinthians 2:10-16
   1 Corinthians 12:3

LINES OF THEOLOGICAL CONNECTION
1. SOTERIOLOGY
   Election
   Grace
   Faith
   Eternal security
   Assurance of salvation

2. PNEUMATOLOGY
   Regeneration
   Illumination

LESSON GLOSSARY
1. Election
   The act of choosing

2. Redeem
   To purchase; to pay a price for

A CHRISTIAN IS ETERNALLY SECURE
BLOCK 6 - THEME 2 - LESSON 4 (188 OF 216)
QUESTIONS

1. According to the Bible, God's salvation is eternal. What weapon does the devil use against us when it comes to being sure of our salvation?

2. Why should we not doubt our salvation?

3. Has the enemy ever caused you to doubt your salvation in Christ? What do you do when you are tempted to doubt?

4. What do you think about God choosing you even before he made the world?

5. Why is the role of the Holy Spirit important in our salvation?

6. Have you believed on Jesus for salvation?

9. SAINTS

THEME: SEEING AS GOD SEES

BLOCK 6 - THEME 3 - LESSON 1

LESSON AIM: Show that a Christian should see themselves as God sees them.

SCRIPTURE: (1 Peter 1:14-16)

"As obedient children, not fashioning yourselves according to the former lusts in your ignorance: But as he which hath called you is holy, so be ye holy in all manner of conversation; Because it is written, Be ye holy; for I am holy."

The Bible uses a word to describe Christians by which many Christians would not consider using to describe themselves. It is the word, "saint". The world has so overused the word and has so misappropriated the word that it has fallen out of the vocabulary of many believers in Christ. We need to get back to using the words the Bible uses of us as God's followers. To do so will help us to see ourselves from God's point of view.

Several words in the New Testament are associated with the word, saint. The words consecration, holy, holiness, purity, piety, sacred, sanctify, and sanctification are near kinsmen to this word and they all apply to us. The words basically mean to set aside for a special purpose.

In the Bible, several kinds of things are said to be holy. Certain places were holy such as cities and buildings and places where God met with people at various times. Things used in the service and worship of God were considered to be holy. And certain people were also holy. All three persons of the Trinity are said to be holy. Angels are called holy. The prophets and apostles were holy. And everyday believers in Christ were holy also.

Holiness has its foundation in God himself. Man has no holiness of his own; he has no holiness in and of himself. Man's holiness comes from the holiness of God. God said, "I am holy, therefore you will be holy." When we believe on Jesus, God begins the work of sanctification; the process of conforming us to the image of Christ. We can also call this the process of making us holy.

When we explore sanctification or holiness, we can consider it in three areas. First our sanctification is positional. This means two things to us. In the first place our position is in Christ. This is that which makes it possible for us to be holy. Since God is holy, and we are in him, we can be holy, too. Second, it means that God has set us aside for his own personal purposes and use. We are his and he can do with us as he wishes. Our passage in 1 Peter goes on to say that God purchased us with the pure, precious blood of Christ. The purity and holiness of Christ has been imputed to us in the same way that Adam's sin was passed on to us. Now, in Christ and through his holiness we are holy as well.

Next, sanctification means that we have a specific purpose for which to live. We are in Christ and God has set us aside for his own use. He intends to use each one of us for his specific purpose. From the Scriptures, we know that God is in the process of rescuing fallen people from every people group on earth. He wants us to join him in this work. He has a specific part that each one of us can play in this work. The pursuit of life is to discover this purpose and to develop it in our lives that we might be deployed to the place and for the work for which God intends to use us. After becoming a Christian, the question becomes, "What does God want me to do now?" We have to search until we have an answer to this question. Then, we have to live our life to fulfill that purpose.

God places within us something which matches his purpose for our life. This something is called desire and it is placed in the deepest, truest part of us, that is, within our heart. The desire of our heart is a clue as to what God's purpose is for our life. Jesus often asked the question to those with whom he came in contact, "What do you want?" This is a legitimate question. Each one of us needs to be free to answer this question before the Lord. Hearing God ask us the question, what do you want, can begin to open the door to discovering the purpose for which God created us and for which we are to give our lives upon this earth. Who doesn't want to know the answer to that? It can all be found when we learn to listen to the desire of our heart. As John Eldredge has said, "Desire reveals design, and design reveals destiny."

Third, sanctification, or holiness is a personal issue. Since God has set us aside and apart for his own purpose and use, we must also set ourselves aside and apart for God's purpose. This is the part in life where we have to make a conscious decision to turn aside from everything that distracts us and draws us away from God, turning to God and to the things he has for us to do. This is a decision that we need to make once and for all and let it be established for the rest of our life. If we do not make it an established principle in our life, it will be easier to give ourselves to the wrong purposes when the time comes in our daily life when we are tempted to turn away from God. If we have consecrated ourselves to the Lord, the Holy Spirit will remind us of this in the hour of temptation. This will make it easier for us to say no to the devil and continue to follow the Lord.

When we have sanctified ourselves to the Lord, we can also sanctify ourselves to his purpose for our life. Jesus did this himself when he was here on the earth. He said that he had committed himself to God's purpose for his life, not only that he might complete his assignment, but also that those who were following him might learn from his example and do the same thing in their life. Here lies the secret to living consistently for the Lord. We must make a commitment to do so and stick to it. If we have personally sanctified ourselves to God for our lifetime and have made this our lifetime commitment, we will be more able to stand for him and keep this commitment in the hour of temptation.

If you are a believer in Christ, God has set you apart for himself. He sees you as holy and he wants you to live a holy life. Tell yourself that God has placed you in him and that he has set you apart for his own personal use. Now, commit yourself to him for that purpose for which he wants you to live your life in Christ.

SAINTS
BLOCK 6 - THEME 3 - LESSON 1 (189 OF 216)
LESSON OUTLINE

Sanctification is:

I POSITIONAL
    A. In Christ
    B. For God's purpose

II PURPOSEFUL
    A. Discover your role
    B. Develop your role

III PERSONAL
    A. A life-time commitment
    B. A moment by moment commitment

SCRIPTURES TO BROADEN YOUR UNDERSTANDING
1. Believers are called saints
    Romans 1:1-7
    1 Corinthians 1:1-2
    2 Corinthians 1:1
    Ephesians 1:1
    Philippians 1:1
    Colossians 1:1-2

2. We belong to God
    1 Corinthians 6:19-20
    1 Peter 1:18-19

3. Christ's sanctification
    John 17:19

LINES OF THEOLOGICAL CONNECTION
1. CHRISTOLOGY
    Christ's sanctification

2. PNEUMATOLOGY
    Sanctification of the believer

3. ANTHROPOLOGY
    Holiness
    The heart's desire
    Life's purpose

LESSON GLOSSARY

1. Consecration
   To set aside as sacred; to devote to a purpose

2. Piety
   Fidelity to obligation; devoutness

3. Sanctification
   To make holy

SAINTS
BLOCK 6 - THEME 3 - LESSON 1 (189 OF 216)
QUESTIONS

1. Where is our foundation for holiness found?

2. In a word, what is the process called for making us holy?

3. What clue has God placed within us to help us find our purpose in life and where do we find it?

4. What question can we ask ourself to begin to discover the desire of our hearts?

5. How would you answer the question, "what do you want?"

6. There is one great practical reason why we need to sanctify ourselves to the Lord. What is it?

7. Have you made a commitment to live your life for God? If not, now is a great time to do so.

10. PURPOSE

THEME: SEEING AS GOD SEES

BLOCK 6 - THEME 3 - LESSON 2

LESSON AIM: God wants us to see his purpose for our lives from his point of view.

SCRIPTURE: (Ephesians 1:17-19)

17 That the God of our Lord Jesus Christ, the Father of glory, may give unto you the spirit of wisdom and revelation in the knowledge of him: 18 The eyes of your understanding being enlightened; that ye may know what is the hope of his calling, and what the riches of the glory of his inheritance in the saints, 19 And what is the exceeding greatness of his power to us-ward who believe, according to the working of his mighty power,

Vision is everything. In the early days of aviation, pilots flew their planes by sight. They used points on the ground as navigation milestones to fly from place to place. When clouds and bad weather rolled in, the planes were grounded simply because the pilots could not see where they were going. They soon began to develop instruments to see for them when they could not see with their natural eye. This has allowed aviation to develop as it has and has saved many a pilot from auguring in, as they say.

Seeing from God's point of view has a similar effect for the Christian. Many times, the clouds of life roll in, obscuring our view of the way we should go and the things we should do in life. We get disoriented easily and lose our way. One of the instruments God has given us to navigate our way through life is to be able to see from God's point of view. From this vantage point, we can see our way clear to travel a greater distance in the work of the Lord.

In this passage of Scripture, Paul reveals to us three essential things we must learn to see from God's point of view. To even do this is possible, we see in the text, because God, the Holy Spirit lives within us. Paul told the Ephesians that he was praying for them, asking the Holy Spirit to turn the light on in their hearts, allowing them to see from God's point of view. Then, he goes on to name these three things we must see from God's perspective.

The first thing we must see from God's point of view is his purpose for our life. It is vital in the church that we begin very early to tell young believers that God has a purpose for their life. If not, the world will soon capture their attention, drawing them away into other pursuits. There are so many wonderful things in the world of interest and worthy of someone's pursuit, but that someone may not be us. These things are not necessarily bad in themselves; it's just that God may not want us to use our time pursuing them. It may be that God has something else in mind for us. This is the thing that we have to determine in life and the only way to do it is to see the purpose of our life from God's point of view.

We have already seen in a previous lesson that when it comes to the purpose of God for our life, there are two areas we must consider. First is the general purpose God has for all believers. We have come to refer to this general purpose with the term, The Great Commission. The Great Commission is the command of the Lord to his followers to make disciples in all nations. This is the goal that every individual Christian should be working toward. It is not an option. It is the one thing God wants every one of us to do. We can do many other things which are good things to do, but if we do them and leave this one thing undone, we have missed God's main purpose for our life in the world.

Once we realize this general purpose God has for our life, we can then begin to ask the question, "How am I going to do this?" The answer to this question will lead us into that second area of consideration; God's specific purpose for our life. The general purpose is the same for all of us. The specific purpose will differ from one of us to the other. You and I may fulfill the commission in two different ways, but they are each acceptable and legitimate if they are the thing God has led us to do and if they get the job done.

There is one clue that God has given us as to what our specific purpose is, and this is the desire of our heart. Often times, when Jesus encountered people, he asked them the question, "What do you want?" To answer this question is to get to the true desire of our heart. Our desire matches the specific purpose God had in mind for us when we were created.

Take some time for yourself and begin to listen to God present the question to you, "What do you want?" The question can be rephrased to ask, "If you could do anything at all as a ministry for God to fulfill his command to make disciples, what would it be?" Almost anything can be made into a ministry of disciple-making. The only things which cannot become ministries are things which God has forbidden in his Word. For example, you cannot make a ministry out of drunkenness, but you can develop a ministry to those who struggle with drunkenness. This is just one example.

Another question you may ask yourself in order to find your specific purpose is: What do I enjoy doing? If there is something you like to participate in, seek ways that you can enjoy it while using it as a ministry at the same time. I once read of a man who loved the sport of fishing. He decided to buy himself a boat and put it on a popular lake in his area and invite men to fish the lake with him. While they were out there, he engaged them in conversations about their relationship with God. He had the opportunity to share the gospel and lead several to Christ. Then, he began to disciple them in order to fulfill the command of the Great Commission. You can do this, too, with anything that you enjoy doing. All you have to do is to find others who enjoy that activity as well and invite them to come along with you. The aim is to develop it into a ministry of disciple-making.

God wants much more from our life than to live it for as many years as we may live only to have little to show for it in terms of the things God really wants. It is essential that we see God's purpose for our life from his point of view. Let's begin our search by praying the prayer Paul prayed, asking God to turn the light on in our heart and let us see the purpose of our life from his perspective.

PURPOSE
BLOCK 6 - THEME 3 - LESSON 2 (190 OF 216)
LESSON OUTLINE

God's purpose for our lives:

I HIS GENERAL PURPOSE
A. The great commission: make disciple sin all nations
B. Not an option

II HIS SPECIFIC PURPOSE
A. Found in the desire of the heart
B. Questions to help discover our desire:
1. How will I fulfill God's general purpose?
2. What do you want?
3. What do I enjoy doing?

SCRIPTURES TO BROADEN YOUR UNDERSTANDING
1. The great commission
Matthew 28:18-20
Acts 1:8
Romans 1:5

2. What do you want?
Matthew 20:21
Matthew 20:32
Mark 10:36

LINES OF THEOLOGICAL CONNECTION
1. ECCLESIOLOGY
The great commission

2. ANTHROPOLOGY
Living for God's purpose
Discovering our spiritual gift

PURPOSE
BLOCK 6 - THEME 3 - LESSON 2 (190 OF 216)
QUESTIONS

1. Why is it possible for us to see from God's point of view?

2. There are many wonderful things in the world to pursue. Why should we be careful about these pursuits?

3. By what term do we refer to God's general purpose for all Christians?

4. What is the great commission?

5. Why is it important to discover the desire of your heart?

6. What do you know about the desire of your heart?

7. What do you enjoy doing from which you could develop a ministry of disciple-making?

11. POTENTIAL

THEME: SEEING AS GOD SEES

BLOCK 6 - THEME 3 - LESSON 3

LESSON AIM: God wants us to see the potential of our lives from his point of view.

SCRIPTURE: (Ephesians 1:17-19)

17 That the God of our Lord Jesus Christ, the Father of glory, may give unto you the spirit of wisdom and revelation in the knowledge of him: 18 The eyes of your understanding being enlightened; that ye may know what is the hope of his calling, and what the riches of the glory of his inheritance in the saints, 19 And what is the exceeding greatness of his power to us-ward who believe, according to the working of his mighty power,

Paul's prayer for vision in this passage covers three vitally important subjects for the believer in Christ. His prayer for the Ephesians, and for us, is that we might see these three things from God's point of view. Through the fall, our vision has been darkened by sin. In the flesh, we are unable to see and approach things from the divine view point. We must have our vision restored. This is our greatest need after we come to Christ.

The first thing Paul prayed that we see from God's perspective is his purpose for our life. We need to know why we are here and what we are supposed to do. This comes from our purpose. Next, he prayed that we will see, as God sees, the potential we have to do something great and significant for God in the world. The third thing is to see the power of God at work in our life. In this study, we will consider two groups of information we need to know about our potential.

Our potential as a believer has to do with our value to God. Paul prayed that we might see the riches of the glory of his inheritance in the saints. Normally, when we hear the word, "inheritance", we assume the Bible is speaking of the inheritance we have awaiting us in heaven. And, it is true that we do have an inheritance awaiting us in heaven. It is on reserve and can never be diminished in any way. However, this is not what Paul is speaking of in this verse. He is not speaking of our inheritance in Christ, but of Christ's inheritance in us. This is a good lesson in how carefully we need to read the Scriptures. If we read the text slowly and think as we read, we will be able to see that Paul is speaking of Christ's inheritance in us.

What does it mean that Christ has an inheritance in us? The Living Bible gives us some insight into this meaning. It says, *"I want you to realize that God has been made rich because we who are Christ's have been given to him!"* Paul is saying that we are part of the reason that God is so rich, and that we are of great value to God. Just how valuable are we to God, we may ask? The answer to this question can be found by considering the price that God paid for us.

When you go into a store to purchase an item of any sort, you know the price range you are willing to pay for that item. If you go into one store and the item seems too high, you go to another store to try to find the same item at a better price. The economic principle is this: the value of any item is not determined by the price tag it has upon it in the store; it is only as valuable as what someone is willing to pay for it. At times, if we really have our heart set on something that we really want, we may even pay a higher price for it simply because it is that valuable to us. This principle applies to the transaction which took place in our redemption. Our value to God is seen in the price God paid for us. And, how much was that? It was Jesus. He gave his all to purchase our redemption. This is our value in the eyes of God: we are worth Jesus Christ. We must see this from God's point of view. To do so will cure any problems we may have with a low self-worth, or a low self-esteem.

We are infinitely valuable to God in Jesus Christ. For this reason, we have a great potential to do something great for God in the world. Christ lives in us and this is our hope of glory. When it comes to potential, we need to understand that it is a moving target. We never finally reach our potential. As we grow and learn and progress, our potential increases. We work out of the new knowledge and experience and wisdom that we gain in life and our potential moves a little farther out in front of us. We journey onward in life, continually growing and reaching forth and our potential increases. We must always pursue it. The more it increases and the more we seem to reach it, we find the more it moves drawing us onward, and the more valuable we continue to become for God and his purpose in the world.

There are many Scripture passages which speak of our potential for God. These passages are worth our study because they tell us more about how much we are all capable of and more of our personal and individual value to God. Our text for this lesson gives us a number of reasons for our need to see this from God's point of view. In this text, we learn that we have potential because God has a purpose for our life. He has designed a place for us in the body of Christ and has equipped us to occupy that place. In that place he has given us a work to do; a reason to exist. We also learn that he is standing by, ready to energize us with his power in order to do the very work he has given us to do. This, too, is a reason that we have unlimited potential. Just think for a moment of all the things you could and would do for God if you knew that you had his power in order to do them. Well, having his power is not an illusion. It is a reality, but there is a catch to it which we will learn in our next lesson.

As a result of the fall, life can often rob us of the glory of our value, or self-worth. Sometimes, people add to our diminishing value by the cruelties of bullying, or name-calling, or some other form of oppression. We may be told that we will never amount to anything. It may be said of us that we are no good to anyone. People unfairly judge us because of any number of reasons from the shape of our body to the color of our skin. These things hurt us and take away from our knowledge of our tremendous value. The truth is, to many people, we may never be of any value. But in the eyes that matter most, in God's eyes, our value is unlimited. In his eyes and in his heart, we are equal in value to his dear Son, the Lord Jesus Christ. When people say or do things to make you feel less valuable, remind yourself that in the sight of the Lord, you are a treasure. And, since you are a treasure unto him, you have the unlimited potential to do significant work for the Lord and leave a lasting spiritual impact in the world. May the Holy Spirit turn the light on in your heart and allow you to see this truth from God's point of view.

POTENTIAL
BLOCK 6 - THEME 3 - LESSON 3 (191 OF 216)
LESSON OUTLINE

I OUR VALUE TO GOD
A. We are Christ's inheritance
B. Our value
C. Potential moves

II REASONS WE HAVE POTENTIAL
A. We are valuable in God's sight
B. God has a purpose for our life
C. God is ready to empower us for his service

SCRIPTURES TO BROADEN YOUR UNDERSTANDING

1. God's Purpose
   Matthew 28:18-20
   Acts 1:8
   2 Timothy 2:2

2. Our value to God
   Deuteronomy 32:10
   John 3:16
   John 15:13
   Romans 5:8
   1 Peter 3:18
   1 John 3:16
   1 John 4:9-10

3. Walking in the light of the Lord
   John 8:12
   Romans 13:12
   Galatians 5:16-26
   Ephesians 4:17-24
   1 Peter 2:9
   2 Peter 3:18
   1 John 1:5-7

4. The fall
   Genesis 3
   Ephesians 2:1-3

5. Vision
   Proverbs 29:18

LINES OF THEOLOGICAL CONNECTION
1. BIBLIOLOGY
   God's Revelation
   The Inspiration of the Scriptures
   Reading the Scriptures
   Interpreting the Scriptures
   Applying the Scriptures Today
   Bible Translations

2. SOTERIOLOGY
   Terms relating to salvation:
   Atonement
   Redemption
   Sanctification (from the spiritual growth aspect)

3. CHRISTOLOGY
   His work of redemption
   The indwelling of Christ in the believer

4. ECCLESIOLOGY
   The body of Christ

5. PNEUMATOLOGY
   The work of illumination
   Spiritual Gifts
   The empowerment of the body of Christ

6. ESCHATOLOGY
   Heaven

POTENTIAL
BLOCK 6 - THEME 3 - LESSON 3 (191 OF 216)
QUESTIONS

1. What is our greatest need after salvation?

2. List the three things Paul prayed that we would see from God's point of view.

3. Potential is related to our _____ to God.

4. In this passage, when Paul uses the word, "inheritance", to what is he referring?

5. From God's point of view, you are equal in value to _____ _____.
   What does this mean to you?

6. What things have happened in your life to rob you of the knowledge and belief that you have value as a person?

7. From the things you listed in question six, what are you willing to let go of in order to see and pursue your potential for God in the world?

8. What steps will you take today to pursue your potential?

12. POWER

THEME: SEEING AS GOD SEES

BLOCK 6 - THEME 3 - LESSON 4

LESSON AIM: God wants us to see from his point of view the power of God that is available to energize us for our mission.

SCRIPTURE: (Ephesians 1:17-19)

17 That the God of our Lord Jesus Christ, the Father of glory, may give unto you the spirit of wisdom and revelation in the knowledge of him: 18 The eyes of your understanding being enlightened; that ye may know what is the hope of his calling, and what the riches of the glory of his inheritance in the saints, 19 And what is the exceeding greatness of his power to us-ward who believe, according to the working of his mighty power,

The Christian's greatest need after salvation is illumination. We have been called out of darkness into the light of Christ, but we have to have our eyes adjusted to the light. To adjust to the light means that we need to be able to see now from God's point of view. This passage reveals three things we must see from God's perspective: his purpose for our life, the potential we have to do something great for God, and the power of God that is available to see that we can accomplish our work for God.

Notice the order of these three life-changing viewpoints. Notice that power comes last in the series. Man's fallen nature wants the order to be reversed. We want the power first. James and John, two of the Lord's disciples, illustrate for us the improper use of God's power. In Luke 9, Jesus had set his face to go to Jerusalem to make the atonement. When the Samaritans did not receive him along the way, James and John were ready to pull the trigger on them and call down fire from heaven to consume them if the Lord so desired. This kind of attitude is one of the reasons Jesus nicknamed them, "the sons of thunder".

Two reasons stand out concerning the misuse of God's power by the sons of thunder. First, they wanted to use the power of God after the manner that had been used by another servant of the Lord. They said, "Do you want us to call down fire from heaven, as Elijah did?" The application of God's power is unique to the servant of God. That which God may want for and through one servant does not always mean this is the way God will use and manifest his power through all of his servants. The experience of God's power is always unique to the servant and to the situation. It is no less the power of God in this way. God and his power are not to be contained in a little box which looks and acts the same for all of us. As we each walk with the Lord, we will see different uses and results from the power of God in and through our life.

The other discrepancy in the proposed use of God's power by James and John has to do with the motive for which it was to be used. James and John were ready to annihilate the Samaritans by using God's power for the wrong purposes. Jesus had to address the motive of their hearts. He said to them, "You do not know what manner of spirit you are of." In other words, he told them the motive of their hearts was wrong, and God will not sanction the use of his power for the wrong motives. He did not come to use his power to destroy people but to deliver them. This is the purpose to which we all must calibrate the use of God's power.

The New Testament employs at least five words to speak in relation to power. These words tell us the way God would have his power operate in and through us. One word is found in Matthew 28:18 in the Great Commission passage where Jesus says that all power (exousia), or authority, has been given to him. The other four words are found in Ephesians 1:19: [power - (dynamis) = ability] [working - (energeia) = action] [mighty - (ischys) = abiding, at home] [power - (kratos) = applied]. When we put these words together in order to determine how God wants to use his power in us, we find that all of God's authority abides in us through his indwelling presence in our life. When this power is applied to our unique personhood and situation, God gives us the ability to act as he would in our given situation.

If the mistakes that the sons of thunder made were not enough when it comes to the power of God, we also make another mistake which may be even greater than theirs. Many times, we do not even call upon this power at all. All of the power of God that will ever be at our disposal already lives within us now that we have been redeemed. There will never be a time when we will have more power than we have right now. The issue is, do we call upon this power when it is needed, or do we try to do the task at hand in our own energy and strength of flesh?

The Bible encourages us to abandon the flesh and call upon the power of God. Concerning our adversary, the Bible tells us to face Satan and his demonic host in the strength and power of the Lord (Ephesians 6:10). The showdown between the sons of Sceva and the demons in Acts 19 is a great example of what can happen when we try to face the enemy in the flesh.

Concerning our work for the Lord, the Bible says that we can do anything the Lord asks us to do in his strength (Philippians 4:13). How many times do we approach our work for the Lord in our own strength and understanding? The Word tells us to not lean upon our own understanding but to acknowledge God in all things that he might give direction for our pathway (Proverbs 3:5-6).

The Bible also tells us that there is no limit whatsoever to what God can and will do through us when we use his power in the right manner, from the right motive, and when we call upon his power in all of our situations (Ephesians 3:20-21). What a shame it is to have all this power living in us in the person of the indwelling Christ and yet be powerless to face the situations at hand, or to accomplish the work God has given us to do.

To see God's power from God's point of view will help us to understand the following truths. As a child of God, all of God's power lives within us right now. If God's power is to be operational within our life, our heart must be in tune with God's heart that his power might be used for his purpose. And, we must call upon this power to be manifested in us and through us to energize us to do God's will. To have God's power will not always mean that seas part in front of us, or that fire rains down from heaven to destroy our enemies. But it will mean that we will be given the help we need, in whatever way God wishes to give it, in order for his will to be accomplished in our life and for his gospel to be advanced to the nations.

POWER
BLOCK 6 - THEME 3 - LESSON 4 (192 OF 216)
LESSON OUTLINE

I AN EXAMPLE OF THE MISUSE OF GOD'S POWER
The Sons of Thunder
A. Wrong manner of use
B. Wrong motive for use

II AN EXPLANATION OF THE USE OF GOD'S POWER
A. Authoritative power
B. Abiding power
C. Applied Power
D. Ability power
E. Active power

SCRIPTURES TO BROADEN YOUR UNDERSTANDING
1. Elijah calls on God's power
   1 Kings 18

2. The Sons of Sceva
   Acts 19:13-20

3. Use of God's power
   Philippians 4:13

4. Christ's power goes beyond our thinking
   Ephesians 3:20-21

LINES OF THEOLOGICAL CONNECTION
1. ANTHROPOLOGY
   Walking in the power of God

2. THE DOCTRINE OF PRAYER
   Calling on God's power through prayer

3. THE DOCTRINE OF SPIRITUAL WARFARE
   Standing in God's power against the devil

POWER
BLOCK 6 - THEME 3 - LESSON 4 (192 OF 216)
QUESTIONS

1. List two areas where James and John intended to use God's power in the wrong way.

2. Why does God not use his power in the same way in all our lives?

3. Have you had an experience of calling on God to empower you to do his will? What happened?

4. What is a great mistake we make concerning the power of God?

13. THE GREAT COMMISSION IS FOR ALL CHRISTIANS

THEME: GOD'S GENERAL PURPOSE

BLOCK 6 - THEME 4 - LESSON 1

LESSON AIM: Show that God's general purpose is the same for every Christian.

SCRIPTURE: (Matthew 28:18-20)

18 And Jesus came and spake unto them, saying, All power is given unto me in heaven and in earth. 19 Go ye therefore, and teach all nations, baptizing them in the name of the Father, and of the Son, and of the Holy Ghost: 20 Teaching them to observe all things whatsoever I have commanded you: and, lo, I am with you alway, even unto the end of the world. Amen.

We often hear that God has a purpose for our life but we do not always hear what that purpose is. People may say, especially after having a close encounter with death, I know God has left me here for a reason, but I do not know what it is. Well, two things are true concerning statements like this: God does have a purpose for our life, and we can know what it is.

It should not come as a surprise that God has revealed his purpose for our lives in the Bible. The Bible is a lamp to our feet and a light to our pathway in life. It is the road map by which we find our way in life. The Holy Spirit guides us according to the Word of God.

Concerning the purpose of God for our life on earth, the Bible tells us that this purpose has two parts. The first part, which is the theme of our lessons this month, has to do with the basic, or general, purpose God has for us. The second part, which we will consider in the next theme, is the specific way each one of us will accomplish the first part.

To begin with, God has a purpose for every Christian, and this purpose is the same. We see this truth in Matthew 28:19a where Jesus said, "Go ye therefore and teach all nations." This is a command, and it gives us the general purpose God has for all of us. The word "ye" is plural and it means all of you, or every one of you. As we are going about the activities of our daily life, we are to teach, or make disciples of all nations. This is God's general purpose for each and every Christian. No Christian is exempted from this purpose.

Many Christians today consider this purpose as if it were an option we can take or leave. This wrong approach to the purpose of God is not entirely their fault. Most Christians have never seen another Christian who fulfills this command, and most Christians have never been personally discipled into becoming the kind of Christian

63

who will fulfill this command. This happens when we fail to follow through with each point within the commission. By the way, this is what we call this passage in the Bible, The Great Commission.

The making of disciples begins with sharing the gospel and leading people to Christ. We call this process evangelism. However, evangelism, in its larger context, includes the work of making the disciple. For too many years, the church has focused on the front part of evangelism, the winning of souls to Christ, but did nothing on the other end to build those who were won into visionary, world-impacting, reproducing disciples of Christ. This is the kind of disciples Jesus meant when he said, make disciples. Christians learned how to present the good news of salvation through Jesus and how to lead a person to Christ, but did not do the work of teaching them what to do or what to become now that they are a Christian. Consequently, our local churches are largely nurseries full of baby Christians. These baby Christians, left to themselves and to figure it out for themselves, struggle their entire lives to know and do God's purpose, most of the time never finding and doing it.

We have to share the gospel in order to win the lost but we have to understand that our work is just beginning when the lost have been won. We are not to win the lost, set them aside as if we have done our job, and move on to win the next one. When the lost are won, we then must begin the work of building that person into a disciple of Christ who is able to do the same work with others and teach them to do the same thing. To do this requires that we are taught and that we also teach the three basic foundation stones of the ministry of making disciples.

The first foundation stone of disciple-making is the mandate. A mandate is a requirement or a command that must be followed. This is what we find in Matthew 28:19a; as you are going, make disciples. This command is given to all Christians and is intended to be fulfilled in the lives of all Christians. This is the reason we say disciple-making is not optional. Jesus fully intends and expects each individual Christian to do this work. It is a mandate for every believer in Christ.

Next, we have the foundation stone of the models of disciple-making in the Bible and elsewhere. There are many examples of the disciple-making relationship within the Word of God. We find disciple-makers in the stories of people like Moses, Joshua, Elijah, Elisha, Peter, Barnabas, Paul, Luke, and Timothy, and others. Of course, the information we have about Jesus is the most comprehensive body of teaching on the process of disciple-making we have in the Bible. In Jesus, we have a number of case studies we can observe to learn many things about how to take a new believer and turn him into a reproducing disciple-maker.

The third foundation stone on which to build a ministry of disciple-making is the method of making disciples that we find in the Bible. There are several steps in this method, and we can see the steps in varying degrees in all of the models we have to examine. At some point, we will specify each step in the disciple-making process, but for now, we will simply point out two important things about the method. One, disciples are made in the context of a relationship. Jesus taught his disciples to watch the people around them and establish a relationship with the ones who seem to give the best opportunity for making a reproducing disciple. Two, within that relationship, all of the information, method, and technique of making disciples can be passed from one person to another. So, disciple-making is done within the relationships we have with others. This opens the door for every Christian to be a disciple-maker because we all have relationships with other people. In this way, Jesus has made it possible for each one of us to make disciples and fulfill his command.

God's general purpose is that each Christian be a maker of disciples. No one is left out of this purpose of God for the Christian and for the church. This is something every Christian can do. It does not require a seminary degree, although it does require a sound Bible knowledge and understanding. It is something which can be done in any environment imaginable. Through it, a Christian can fulfill The Great Commission. He can multiply his own life, increasing the impact of his individual life in the world. Through disciple-making, the message of the gospel and its transforming power can be carried to all the peoples of the world. It is the general purpose God has for all of us. The only thing that makes sense is to learn it, live it, and lead others to do the same thing. Have you been discipled, and are you making disciples?

THE GREAT COMMISSION IS FOR ALL CHRISTIANS
BLOCK 6 - THEME 4 - LESSON 1 (193 OF 216)
LESSON OUTLINE

Foundation stones for a ministry of disciple-making

I THE MANDATE
A. Jesus commanded us to make disciples of the nations
B. This command is not optional

II THE MODELS
A. Old and New Testament models
B. Jesus is our greatest model

III THE METHOD
A. Disciples are made in the context of a relationship
B. All method and technique should be employed in our personal relationships

SCRIPTURES TO BROADEN YOUR UNDERSTANDING
1. God's original plan to multiply
   Genesis 1:28

2. The theme of the Bible
   Genesis 3:15

3. Evangelism and disciple-making are connected to the Bible's theme
   2 Corinthians 5:14-21

4. Jesus' disciple-making encounters
   Matthew 4:12-20
   Matthew 9:9-17
   John 1:29-51

John 3
John 4
John 21:15-25
To name a few

5. A prayer for purpose
Ephesians 1:15-19

LINES OF THEOLOGICAL CONNECTION
1. THE DOCTRINE OF THE SCRIPTURES
The Bible's theme of redemption through Jesus Christ
Evangelism and disciple-making are connected to the Bible's theme

2. DISCIPLE-MAKING
Bible models of disciple-making
Jesus strategy of disciple-making

3. ANTHROPOLOGY
God's purpose for your life

LESSON GLOSSARY
1. Mandate
An authoritative command

2. Commission
The authority to act as an agent for another

THE GREAT COMMISSION IS FOR ALL CHRISTIANS
BLOCK 6 - THEME 4 - LESSON 1 (193 OF 216)
QUESTIONS

1. Write out God's general purpose for every Christian and its Bible reference.

2. What is the label we have given this purpose of God for our lives?

3. Is any Christian exempt from fulfilling the great commission?

4. What is the simple answer as to why Christians do not obey the great commission?

5. Where does disciple-making begin?

6. As a student in the LIFE Plan, you are being discipled with the necessary tools that will enable you to fulfill God's general purpose for your life. Will you make a personal commitment to God that you will learn this information and obey his commission?

7. God fully expects you to be a maker of disciples. Think about your present relationships. Who do you know right now that you can begin to disciple?

8. You come into contact everyday with people you do not know. Of these, who is God leading you to begin a personal relationship with that can be used for making disciples?

14. THE GREAT COMMISSION IS TIED TO A PROMISE

THEME: GOD'S GENERAL PURPOSE

BLOCK 6 - THEME 4 - LESSON 2

LESSON AIM: Show that the promise of God's presence with us is dependent upon our obedience to his commission.

SCRIPTURE: (Matthew 28:18-20)

18 And Jesus came and spake unto them, saying, All power is given unto me in heaven and in earth. 19 Go ye therefore, and teach all nations, baptizing them in the name of the Father, and of the Son, and of the Holy Ghost: 20 Teaching them to observe all things whatsoever I have commanded you: and, lo, I am with you alway, even unto the end of the world. Amen.

For forty days following the resurrection of the Lord Jesus Christ from the dead, Jesus went in and out among his disciples. That is, he appeared and disappeared in and from their presence, apparently time and again. They might be in a locked room and all of a sudden, Jesus would appear in their presence. He spoke to them, ate fish with them, and was gone just as suddenly as he had appeared. What was his purpose in doing this? He wanted them to be aware of his presence with them when they could not see him as much as they were aware of it when they could see him. For the previous three years, Jesus had been with them constantly, nearly every day and night. Now, he was going away. They would not see him every day any more. But, this did not change the fact that he would be with them still, even if they were not able to physically see him.

When we think of the presence of God with us as his children, we must consider it in the two ways that this subject is presented to us in the Bible. In the first place, God has promised to be with those who believe on him. The very first reason the Bible states for the calling of the disciples of Jesus was that they might be with him. The presence of the Lord with us is one of the crucial doctrines of the faith. We are not alone, even when we are alone. We may be faced in life with all kinds of situations when people cannot be with us, either physically or practically or personally. There will be times when we will have to face problems and make decisions alone. We have the comfort and assurance from the Scriptures that in these times, God will be with us.

God is with us through salvation. When we are born again, God indwells us. He takes up a residence within us. He lives in our spirit. In fact, this is what the new birth is: it is a resurrection of our spirit which died when Adam sinned. Regeneration, as it is called in theology, is the work of the Holy Spirit and happens as God moves into our spirit. Since he lives within us, he can fulfill his promise to be with us from now on. He has promised to never leave us nor forsake us. So, the very first consideration in the presence of God with us has to do with salvation. The presence of God with us guarantees us that once we are saved, we can never again be unsaved. Our salvation is eternal. This is underscored again in one of the very first names the Bible gives for Jesus. He is called Emmanuel which means, God with us.

The second consideration concerning the presence of God with us has to do with another subject entirely. It has to do with our service to God. God has given us a huge assignment in the world. He has commissioned us to take the news of salvation through Jesus to all the nations of the world. Nations in this context refers to the peoples of the world, not to geographical boundaries. There as some 12,000 distinct people groups in the world. About half of them are considered unreached with the gospel. This means that they have never heard of Jesus and that he died for them on the cross, and that through him they can have eternal life. We have been given the task of taking this news throughout the world.

One might think that to receive such news would be welcomed and that those who hear it for the first time ever would instantly receive the news and believe and be saved. However, it is not that simple. These people groups have had centuries of false belief and idol worship which has such a hold in their lives and such a grip on their hearts that they are reluctant and often afraid to forsake all they have ever known to believe this news that sounds too good to be true. To believe, for them, is to forsake much of their history and way of life. It is not an easy decision.

It is into these situations that God is sending his followers to take the good news of salvation through Jesus Christ. To go into these places and situations can often be dangerous and hostile. Many have lost their lives for doing so. But, God has promised to be with us as we undertake this kingdom work. He will be with us into the hostile arenas of life and will face with us whatever opposition may come our way. He does not promise that our lives will always be spared as we do his work. He does promise that he will be with us to the very last step we take, whatever that may be.

This is the subject of the Bible text for this lesson. Jesus said, "I will be with you to the end of the world". When we look at the passage as a whole, we do not have the liberty to separate the promise of his presence with us from the purpose he has for us. He began by stating his purpose for us: as you are going about your normal routine of life, make disciples of all nations. Then he connected his promise to be with us to this mission. This means that, in this context, if we want to claim the presence of God with us in our service to him, we must fulfill the assignment he has given to us. We cannot ignore his assignment and claim his promise at the same time. These two things are inseparable.

Many churches are suffering today and struggling to stay afloat. When you visit these churches, there is often the obvious sense that the presence of God is nowhere in the vicinity of the church. If you look deeply enough into the reason for this in each individual case, you will most likely discover one of two scenarios. Either they have never had a true vision for fulfilling the Lord's commission to make disciples in all nations, or, at some point along the way, they have forsaken this assignment for some form of a substitute. In either case, God is not obligated to manifest his presence among them. When the church refuses to do the works that God wants them to do, he refuses to manifest his presence in that place.

It is a fact that God comes into the lives of those who truly believe on him in their hearts and he will never leave them. But if they will not follow him to the work, he will not show himself to, or through these people. He will look for those who are willing to follow him to the ends of the earth and he will fulfill his promise to be with us to them. In summary, Jesus is with us because in salvation. He wants to also be with us in our faithful and obedient service to him in the fulfillment of his great commission to make disciples in all nations. If you are a believer, God lives within you and will never leave. If you will be obedient to his commission, you will experience the presence of God with you as you can experience in no other way. Take him at his word. Do the work he wants you to do. In doing so, you can legitimately claim his promise of this presence with you to the end of the earth, until the end of time.

THE GREAT COMMISSION IS TIED TO A PROMISE
BLOCK 6 - THEME 4 - LESSON 2 (194 OF 216)
LESSON OUTLINE

God's presence with us:

I IN SALVATION
    A. God's promised presence
    B. God indwells us

II IN SERVICE
    A. God's purpose for us is to take the good news to all people
    B. God will manifest himself to those who are fulfilling his purpose

SCRIPTURES TO BROADEN YOUR UNDERSTANDING
1. Things people suffered to follow Christ
    Hebrews 11
    2 Corinthians 11

2. God's promise to never leave us
    Hebrew 13:5
    Romans 8:33-39

3. God's purpose for us
    Mark 3:14
    Matthew 28:18-20
    Acts 1:8

LINES OF THEOLOGICAL CONNECTION
1. CHRISTOLOGY
   God with us
   Manifests himself to his followers

2. ANTHROPOLOGY
   Fulfilling God's purpose
   Obeying even in opposition
   Suffering for the sake of the gospel

THE GREAT COMMISSION IS TIED TO A PROMISE
BLOCK 6 - THEME 4 - LESSON 2 (194 OF 216)
QUESTIONS

1. What was Jesus' purpose in appearing and disappearing before the disciples in the days following his resurrection?

2. What is another term for regeneration?

3. What is regeneration, or, the new birth?

4. What does the name Emmanuel mean?

5. What is the main reason God's presence cannot be experienced in some churches?

6. Do you experience a lack of the presence of God in your life? Why do you think this is?

15. TO EVANGELIZE ALL NATIONS

THEME: GOD'S GENERAL PURPOSE

BLOCK 6 - THEME 4 - LESSON 3

LESSON AIM: Show that evangelism is the first step fulfilling the great commission.

SCRIPTURE: (Mark 16:15)

And he said unto them, Go ye into all the world, and preach the gospel to every creature.

The root command within the great commission is to make disciples of all nations. No matter where we find them, across the sea or across the street, every ethnic group is a target toward which we are to aim the gospel of the Lord Jesus Christ. Making disciples is the command of the commission, but in order to do this, it must be preceded by evangelism. Evangelism and disciple-making are opposite sides of the same coin. If we are to make disciples, we have to evangelize. And if we evangelize, we are to make disciples of the evangelized. We need both.

"Go into all the world and preach the gospel to every creature." This looks good on paper and it is so easy to repeat. It sounds like such an awesome mission statement for the church or the Christian who wants to do the will and work of the Lord. When we observe the facts, however, we find that very few Christians and churches are actually doing it to any measurable degree. We are told that less than two percent of Christians are involved in the ministry of evangelism. Some eighty percent do not share a verbal witness for Christ on a consistent basis. And, ninety five percent of all Christians have never won a single soul to Christ. There seems to be a huge gap between the Lord's command to evangelize the nations and our obedience to do so. Let's try to learn why this is so as we consider some of the factors involved in the work of evangelism.

To begin with, we must admit that the task is enormous from the numbers alone. Every single person who is born into the world is born in a condition of condemnation and separation from God due to sin. Today, of the more than seven billion people on the earth, 2.2 billion claim to be Christian. This leaves 4.9 billion, at least, to be without God. This is a lot of people to whom the church must preach the gospel.

The next factor we have to think about are the groups in which these numbers of people find themselves. We call them, people groups. And, there are some 16,761 different, distinct people groups on earth. This represents many cultural barriers which have to be overcome in order to get to the billions of individuals living among these people groups. About 7,000 of these groups are considered to be unreached with the gospel. This means that less than two percent of them have heard and believed the good news about salvation through Jesus.

Then there are the languages barriers. There are about 7,000 languages spoken on the earth today. Some of these languages are dead or dying languages. Some of them are spoken languages only and have no alphabet. No one reads the language. The gospel can be shared with these people and they can be won to Christ by hearing the message, but disciple-making is hampered by their inability to read the Bible in their own language. Many of the languages do not have the Bible or any portion of it in the language. Someone has to live among these people, learn their language, create an alphabet, translate the Scriptures, and teach them to read. Then, they can begin the work of teaching the Bible to them and of teaching them how to understand what it means in order for them to teach it to others. This all takes much time and lots of hard work.

There is also the accessibility of the people. Some of them live in remote villages of the world's jungles or mountains. To get to them requires long hours of travel to reach them. A worker may make several flights, vehicle rides by car, bus or train, boat rides, and then still walk or ride an animal to get to the village. And, once they get there, there may be hostility toward the outsider that hinders or prevents altogether his or her ministry among the people. Those who go to these people and places go at the risk of their own life many times. These and other problems as well are factors which make the work of evangelism a difficult assignment indeed.

Furthermore, there are the obstacles within the church which has the task of evangelizing the nations of the world. The first obstacle is to win the battle over one's own flesh in order to obey God's command. Obedience is costly, and there is a great inner battle to win for those who will obey. Few are willing to obey and surrender to this degree. This cuts down the work force considerably. And, there are the resources. Where will the money come from in order to do this work? How will we live? How will we support our families? All of these factors, among the nations and within the church, work together to make the church less likely to engage in the work of evangelism on this level. Frankly, many Christians are not willing to pay this high of a cost to do the work of evangelism. In fact, we even find it hard to share the gospel with our families, co-workers, friends and neighbors who live within our reach and without the barriers we have mentioned. It is much easier, disobedient as it may be, to mind our own business, enjoy our salvation, and not think very much about the masses that are going to hell at the rate of 70,000 per day from unreached people groups in these hard to reach places around the world.

Jesus did not promise us that the work would be easy. He did not promise that the work would not require great sacrifice and suffering for the ones who obey his command. After all, look at what it cost him. He did tell us to do it, and that we could count on him to be with us as we do it. He also promised that others would believe as we do the work. We, as Christians, must humble ourselves and ask God to help us be obedient to his command. The resources are available already if we will obey. It is our own pride and disobedience that stands in the way of our getting the job done.

It is said that there are 900 churches for every unreached people group in the world. There are 78,000 Evangelical Christians for each unreached people group. The church worldwide has about 9,000 times the work force and 3,000 times the financial resources to get the job done. In fact, 0.03% of the income of Evangelical Christians could plant the church in all of the world's unreached people groups. What then is the problem? Why is the job still unfinished?

Doing the work and completing the task comes down to the obedience of the individual Christian. What sacrifices are you willing to make? What work are you willing to do to help evangelize the people of the world who have not yet heard the good news of salvation through Jesus Christ? Ask God what he wants you to do, what course of action does he want you to take. Make the commitment to take this course of action. And, keep your eyes on the goal for the rest of your life. Do your part to preach the gospel to every creature on earth as the Lord has commanded us all to do.

TO EVANGELIZE ALL NATIONS
BLOCK 6 - THEME 4 - LESSON 3 (195 OF 216)
LESSON OUTLINE

Hindering factors to the work of evangelism:

I AMONG THE PEOPLES
   A. People groups
   B. Languages
   C. No Bible in some languages
   D. Accessibility
   E. Approachability

II WITHIN THE CHURCH
   A. Obedience
   B. Small work force
   C. Resources

SCRIPTURES TO BROADEN YOUR UNDERSTANDING
1. Preach the gospel
   Romans 1:16
   Romans 10:8-15
   1 Corinthians 1:17-24
   Ephesians 2

LINES OF THEOLOGICAL CONNECTION
1. SOTERIOLOGY
   The power of the gospel to save

2. PNEUMATOLOGY
   Regeneration

3. DISCIPLE-MAKING
   Evangelism
   Disciple-making strategy

4. ANTHROPOLOGY
   People groups
   Unreached people groups

TO EVANGELIZE ALL NATIONS
BLOCK 6 - THEME 4 - LESSON 3 (195 OF 216)
QUESTIONS

1. What is the number one reason why we should share the gospel with the lost?

2. List some obstacles to sharing the gospel.

3. When you think about the billions who are without God in the world, what can you do to help the situation?

4. Have you ever personally won a soul to Christ by sharing the gospel with them?

5. Do you know anyone personally who needs to know Christ? Who are they, and are you willing to share the gospel with them?

6. How does evangelism and disciple-making work together?

7. What is the greatest reason so many people are still without God in the world?

8. Will you be willing to set a goal to win at least one person to God?

16. TO DISCIPLE THE NATIONS

THEME: GOD'S GENERAL PURPOSE

BLOCK 6 - THEME 4 - LESSON 4

LESSON AIM: Show that we are to disciple the evangelized into the great commission.

SCRIPTURE: (Romans 1:5)

By whom we have received grace and apostleship, for obedience to the faith among all nations, for his name:

God has blessed the United States of America. American technological advances and know how have helped to make life better for many people around the world. Our military has led the charge for freedom all across the globe. And the church in America has done much to take the gospel of Christ to the nations. America and Americans, having been blessed of God, have been a blessing in many ways and in many places all over the earth. Because of this, it can be easy for us as Christians to think that we are the ones doing all the work for Christ in the world. We must remember that even as much as we have done, we are only a part of the whole process. We join with believers of all nations to do the work. We must remember that other nations and the work they do is just as important as ours.

God has given his commission to his church. This includes all the nations. The church is made up of believers from many different tribes, tongues, kindred, and nations on the earth. The assignment that God has given to the church is the same for all people groups. We are all to make disciples of all nations. Every ethnic group needs to be trained in the work of disciple-making in order to get the job done. There are a number of reasons for this.

The first reason the nations must be trained in the work of disciple-making, obviously, is because this is exactly what Christ commanded us to do. His commission is to make disciples of all nations. God's plan is that someone from every ethnic group on earth will be saved and will be with him throughout eternity. John, writing of the future which had been revealed to him, saw this throng of people in heaven with God. Between now and then, we are to continue telling the story of Jesus around the world, taking the gospel to the nations who have not yet heard his good news. Once people are born into God's family, we are to train them to do this same work among their own people and among other nations as well.

The nations are to be discipled to reach the nations because they can do the best job of reaching their own people. There are as many different cultures as there are different peoples in the world. Culture is the way a people experiences and responds to the world in which they live. Culture can be a barrier that hinders the spread of the gospel. What better person could impact a given culture than one who has become a believer within that culture? This person knows the culture and can use it as a means to help communicate the gospel rather than having it be an obstacle. Those Christians outside the culture have to learn enough about it before they can communicate within it. The indigenous person is the best candidate to spread the gospel and make disciples within a given culture.

We are to disciple the nations to be disciples of the nations also because they may have access to nations that are not accessible to some other peoples. For example, 60% of unreached people groups live in countries which are closed to missionaries from North America. North American Christians would not be able to reach them, but the peoples within their own countries or from certain other countries would have access to them. God anticipated this problem, therefore, all the nations were given the same commission. For one nation that might be forbidden access to a particular people group, there may be a dozen others who would have access to them. In this way, our adversary is unable to stop the spread of the gospel merely be keeping one or several people groups out of the fields of harvest.

The nations are to be discipled to disciple the nations also that they might have the privilege of joining God in the work he is doing. God is no respecter of persons. He wants all of his people to work with him as co-laborers in the fields. All nations have this privilege. All people bear the image of God and reflect his glory. There is no greater way to celebrate the diversity of people and to recognize their uniqueness than the way these are on display when the nations join God in his mission to tell the good news of the Savior to the world.

Finally, we are to disciple the nations to disciple the nations because the Lord's strategy of disciple-making is adaptable to all peoples. There is not a place, or a people, or a setting where this strategy will not work. This is part of the genius of the plan. The plan itself is simple and easily reproducible. Anyone can follow it and reproduce a reproducing disciple. But, the fact that it will work among any people on earth also makes the strategy successful.

When Adam fell into sin in the Garden of Eden, the entire human race fell as well. Every person born into the world enters the world separated from God. We refer to this condition as being "lost". This condition applies to all individuals of all people groups. After the fall, God promised that he would send a deliverer to rescue people from every ethnic group from this fallen, or sinful condition. Jesus Christ was that deliverer that God had promised. Jesus came, died on the cross as a sacrifice for our sin, was buried and arose from the dead. Through his death and life again, he is able to rescue people from their lost condition. God does this rescuing work, but he has given his followers the privilege and assignment of telling the story of what he has done to all the peoples of the world. This telling the story is what we call evangelism. When people believe in Christ as a result of being evangelized, those who evangelize them are to teach and train them to do the same thing with others which has been done with them. They now become the evangelists and the disciple-makers for other people. They are to engage in the same process of witnessing of Christ, winning souls, and making disciples. Those whom they reach are to be taught to do the same things. This is how we make reproducing disciples who can make an impact in the world for Christ.

At some point, you as an individual Christian must get involved in this process. It is the will of God that those whom he has saved would become disciple-makers. God has provided everything we need in order to do this work. He gave us several examples in the Bible from which we can learn. In Jesus, he gave us not only the perfect model of a disciple-maker, but he also gave us the strategy, or method, to use by which we can make disciples. Every Christian on earth should have this privilege to do this work. This is the method God has given us so that our life can make a real difference in the world for his sake. Are you learning the method, are you using it, and are you teaching others to use it, especially those who are of a different ethnic group than you?

TO DISCIPLE THE NATIONS
BLOCK 6 - THEME 4 - LESSON 4 (196 OF 216)
LESSON OUTLINE

Reasons all nations must make disciples:

I CHRIST COMMANDED IT
A. All nations are to be discipled
B. All nations are to make disciples

II THE NATIONS CAN DO THE BEST JOB OF REACHING THEIR OWN PEOPLE
A. Outsiders have to learn the culture
B. Insiders already know the culture

III SOME PEOPLES HAVE BETTER ACCESS TO OTHER PEOPLES
A. Some nations have no access to certain peoples
B. Some nations have access that other nations may not have

IV THE NATIONS GET TO JOIN GOD IN HIS WORK
A. All nations have the privilege to work with God
B. This is the best way to reflect God's glory

V THE DISCIPLE-MAKING STRATEGY IS ADAPTABLE TO ALL PEOPLE
A. The strategy is simple
B. All peoples can use it

SCRIPTURES TO BROADEN YOUR UNDERSTANDING
1. All nations in heaven
   Revelation 5:9

2. The lost condition
   Ephesians 2:1-3

3. We have all we need in order to make disciples
   2 Timothy 1:9-10

4. Making disciples of the nations is commanded by Jesus
   Matthew 28:19

LINES OF THEOLOGICAL CONNECTION
1. THE DOCTRINE OF SIN
   What it means to be lost
   Total depravity

2. CHRISTOLOGY
   Redeemer
   The gospel

3. THE DOCTRINE OF GOD
   God's redemptive plan

4. ANTHROPOLOGY
   Cross-cultural ministry
   Missions

LESSON GLOSSARY
1. Culture
   Culture is the way a people experiences and responds to the world in which they
   Live

2. Indigenous
   Living naturally in a particular region

TO DISCIPLE THE NATIONS
BLOCK 6 - THEME 4 - LESSON 4 (196 OF 216)
QUESTIONS

1. How many different cultures are there in the world?

2. From an evangelistic perspective, what is so important about a people's culture?

3. What are some cultural peculiarities about your culture?

4. How would your answer from the previous question help or hinder someone sharing the gospel with you?

5. Have you had any interaction with anyone from another ethnic group?

6. What are some of the cultural differences you have noted between them and you?

7. Have you tried to share the gospel of Jesus Christ with them?

8. Have you discovered anything about their culture that could be an inroad for the gospel into their life?

17. TWO REASONS YOU WERE SAVED

THEME: GOD'S SPECIFIC PURPOSE

BLOCK 6 - THEME 5 - LESSON 1

LESSON AIM: Show two practical reasons why we were saved.

SCRIPTURE: (Mark 3:14)

And he ordained twelve, that they should be with him, and that he might send them forth to preach.

When God saved us, he had a purpose in mind for each one of us. This purpose is two-fold. One part of this purpose is the same general purpose for all of us. God intends that each believer in Christ work toward the same goal. This goal is the same goal God himself is working toward. We are told in Genesis 3:15 that God has been working to bring his Savior to the world who will not only rescue the fallen but will also destroy the works of the devil in the process. Now that the Savior has come and has died and has risen from the dead, believers are to join God in this rescue mission by taking the gospel to the nations, evangelizing them and making disciples of the evangelized. This is the general purpose God has for our lives.

The other part of God's purpose is the specific purpose he has for each one of us as individuals. This specific purpose is the particular way we will each go about the business of fulfilling God's general purpose in our own life. Mark 3:14 speaks of this dual purpose with an added dimension that we must consider.

As Jesus began his public ministry, he worked alone for a period of time. As he went from place to place doing the work of teaching, preaching, healing and other things, Jesus paid attention to the people who followed him in the crowds. From the crowds Jesus hand-picked several men who would be his close companions for the next couple of years. As he chose them, he intended to train them and turn over his ministry to them at some point in the near future. He knew that he would not be with them very long so he prepared them for his coming departure. This preparation is what we know to be the work of disciple-making and spiritual reproduction.

Our Scripture verse tells us two objectives Jesus had in mind when he chose these men. As God calls out believers today from the world, he has the same two objectives in mind. He had the same objectives in mind when he called each one of us. We can also say that these are two reasons, from God's perspective, why we were saved.

First, God selected these men and us so that we could be with him. Now, we know that when this life is over, we are going to be with Jesus where he is. However, this is not what the Bible is referring to in this passage. Jesus is speaking of being with him in terms of a personal relationship. He is speaking of the time we need to spend in private with God as a believer in Christ. He is speaking of the time we spend with God reading the Bible, meditating on the Word, in prayer, and in trying to discern God's will and plan for our life. As the verse tells us that Jesus called his disciples to be with him, it is speaking of the fact that God wants each one of his followers to have a personal, deep, and intimate relationship with him.

In our personal relationship with God using the Bible, prayer, and depending upon the Holy Spirit to help and teach us, God reveals more and more of himself to us. At the same time, he also lets us see ourselves as we are in his sight: fallen, coming short of his glory, powerless within ourselves, unrighteous in our own right. In this relationship, he leads us to surrender who we are to all that we learn about who he is. And, as we do, Jesus becomes more and more able to live his life through ours in the way that he wants to, free from the selfish desires that our flesh would use to obstruct God's will in our lives. In this way, God is at work to recondition us according to his will. He works to mold us and form us after the image of his Son, Jesus. He is working to make us think, act, and live just like Jesus would if he were still living on this earth. As a matter of fact, Jesus does continue to live on the earth and he lives through his followers who are surrendered to him. This process of being with Jesus is a process of preparing us to find and follow the specific purpose God has for our lives.

Second, Jesus chose us that he might send us on the mission he intends for us to do. As we have already stated, this mission is to take the gospel of Jesus Christ to the nations of the world. Each one of us, in our private time with Jesus, will have to discover the specific way he wants us to accomplish this work. He wants us to develop a personal ministry for him out of the discovery we make concerning God's specific purpose for our lives.

A ministry for the Lord's purpose of preaching the gospel to the nations and making disciples of those who believe can be developed from just about anything you can imagine. The key is to ask yourself questions like these: If I could do anything for the Lord as a ministry, what would it be? What is it that I love to do? What is it that I am good at? What is the spiritual gift I have been given by the Holy Spirit? The answers to these questions can help you begin to determine and develop a ministry of disciple-making for the Lord. If you like music, for example, and all the disciplines which go with it, from it you can build a personal ministry for the Lord. The same is true for just about everything else: writing, art, sports, acting, building, cooking, sewing, flying, medicine, science, English, and millions of other things. God wants us to explore and be creative in our work for him. We all may do something totally different as a ministry and it is all good if through them we are getting disciples made in all nations as God commanded.

As we go about being with Jesus and being sent for him, we need to keep these two things in mind. Our private life with God prepares us for our life in public for God. And, our public life for God will never rise above our private life with God. This simply means that if we spend little to no time with God in private, we cannot expect him to be able to use us to any great extent in the public arena. Keep in mind that it is in the private time with God that he prepares us for our public life on his behalf. On the other hand, if we have a strong and meaningful relationship with God in which we are learning and growing and seeking his will, he is going to show us that will and how it can be accomplished in our life.

This lesson is one of the greatest lessons you will ever learn in your lifetime. It is one of the keys to a life well lived for the Lord. It can prepare you for a lifetime of wonderful time spent with God and in service for him that can have an impact both in the world and upon the world. Learn at a young age to practice each day both of these intentions God has for you. Spend time with him in private. Work for him in the public life out of what he gives you in your private time with him. To do so will mean the difference in a life lived, even perhaps for many years but with very little done of eternal significance, and a life lived, although but for a short span of time, but lived according to God's will. To live in this way will match the intentions God had in mind when he called you to be his child.

TWO REASONS YOU WERE SAVED
BLOCK 6 - THEME 5 - LESSON 1 (197 OF 216)
LESSON OUTLINE

I OUR PRIVATE LIFE WITH GOD - GOD SAVED US TO BE WITH HIM
    A. An intimate relationship with God
    B. God prepares us for his specific purpose for our life

II OUR PUBLIC LIFE FOR GOD - GOD SAVED US TO SEND US
    A. God has a general purpose for all of us: make disciples of all nations
    B. God has a specific purpose for all of us: the way we will each make disciples
        1. Discover how God has equipped you
        2. Develop a personal ministry of disciple-making from almost anything

SCRIPTURES TO BROADEN YOUR UNDERSTANDING
1. God's purpose in the world
   Genesis 3:15

2. The great commission
   Matthew 28:18-20

3. Jesus' disciple-making strategy
   John 17

LINES OF THEOLOGICAL CONNECTION
1. PNEUMATOLOGY
   The spiritual gifts

2. THE DOCTRINE OF GOD
   God's general purpose for all of us
   God's specific purpose for each of us

3. ANTHROPOLOGY
   Developing a personal ministry
   Personal evangelism
   The desire of the heart

TWO REASONS YOU WERE SAVED
BLOCK 6 - THEME 5 - LESSON 1 (197 OF 216)
QUESTIONS

1. According to Genesis 3:15, what is the work of Jesus in the world?

2. In what two ways can we consider God's purpose for our lives on earth?

3. What is the difference between God's general purpose and his specific purpose?

4. List the two reasons why God saved us.

5. What does it mean, "to be with God"?

6. What two additional things do we need to remember from this lesson?

7. Do you spend time with God on an individual basis?

8. Do you have an idea of God's specific purpose for your life?

18. GOD'S SPECIFIC PURPOSE FOR THE BELIEVER'S LIFE

THEME: GOD'S SPECIFIC PURPOSE

BLOCK 6 - THEME 5 - LESSON 2

LESSON AIM: Present the fact that God has a specific plan for the individual life of each believer.

SCRIPTURE: (Romans 12:1-2)

¹ I beseech you therefore, brethren, by the mercies of God, that ye present your bodies a living sacrifice, holy, acceptable unto God, which is your reasonable service. ² And be not conformed to this world: but be ye transformed by the renewing of your mind, that ye may prove what is that good, and acceptable, and perfect, will of God.

Everyone wants to know that his or her life matters. We want to know that our being here on earth made a difference and that we meant something to someone. We search not only for the meaning of life in general, but for the meaning of our life in particular. And we typically search in all the wrong places for this so great a treasure. Unfortunately, many believers in the church live their lifetime without ever knowing specifically why they are here.

One of the most frustrating and helpless feelings in the world is the feeling of insignificance. The daily grind of life amplifies the inner gnawing to find the life we prize. We get up and go through the motions of survival every day, wanting to have significance, but somehow missing it in the steady plodding of everyday life. We get up; we go to work; we wash our clothes; we eat our food; we pay the bills; we go to bed; and we do it all again tomorrow. Where, in the continuous cadence of life, is the significance for which we were made, and for which we long?

Why am I here? What is the specific purpose for my life? The Bible gives us the clues we need to answer this question for ourselves. And this is what we have to do: we have to find the answer to the question for ourselves. No one can answer the question for us. Others can point us to the clues, but we have to find the answer for ourselves. And, if we ever find it, we will find the answer somewhere along the way in the journey of our lives. Remember when God called Abram out of Ur, he told him to leave everything behind and go to a place that he would show him. This is the basic calling that everyone feels in their life. Only those who are willing to take up the journey will find their answer.

We have said that God has a general purpose for the life of every believer in the Lord Jesus Christ. This is his purpose that we all make disciples of the nations. God also has a specific purpose for each one of us. The specific purpose is how we, as an individual, will fulfill the general purpose. That is, how we will go about the work of making disciples of Christ. Our Scripture passage is one of the Bible's starting places for us to begin our journey to find the specific purpose God has for our life. It contains a number of important elements for the journey.

To begin with, writing to the Romans, Paul tells us that God does have a specific purpose for our lives. He calls it, "the will of God". He gives us three details about the will of God for our lives. First, he says it is good, or beneficial to us, to find and fulfill the will of God. Knowing and doing the will of God means the difference between a life invested into the purpose of God, or a life lived on earth, perhaps for many years, but ultimately wasted if we never come to know that specific thing God intended for us to do.

Next, Paul says the will of God is acceptable. This simply means that the purpose that God has is fully agreeable, or perfectly suitable to us as an individual. God created us. He knows us inside and out. The part he has chosen for us to play in the story he is telling is a role written with us in mind. God has taken the care to equip us for this role so that when we find it, it will feel like a perfect fit for us. This is also one of the ways that confirms that we have found it, when we feel like we are doing that thing for which we were made.

Third, Paul says the will of God for us is perfect. The word, perfect, here means complete. In the specific purpose of God for us, nothing is lacking. This is that built in factor that helps prevent us from straying off the course into the insignificant. If there is nothing lacking in God's will for our life, we do not have to try to find what we desire in any other place. We can continue in the direction that God wants for us, knowing that everything we need will be in this direction. The word, perfect, also carries the idea of full age. It is only when we find the specific purpose that God has for our life that we can grow and mature and become all that God wants us to be. To not know God's purpose is to be immature as a believer. Already, we can see what a wonderful thing it is to know God's will for our lives. These verses reveal that everything that we truly need and desire is to be found in the purpose of God.

We have three basic responsibilities to the will of God in our lives. In the first place, we have to prove it. To prove the will of God just means that we have to discover it, or find out what it is. Later in this chapter, Paul gives us the seven basic categories of spiritual gifts. Every believer has at least one spiritual gift. The gift is also one of the clues we have to help us make the discovery of the specific purpose of God for our life. It is our gift which prepares us for the work we are to do. It can be a help to discovering our specific purpose in life.

A second responsibility we have toward the will of God for our life is that we overcome the obstacles in life that prevent God's will from being accomplished. The particular obstacle Paul addresses in the text is the subtle and steady drawing of the world away from God's will. The kind of command Paul uses in the verse is the kind of command that tells us to stop an action that is already happening. The Phillips translation says, "Stop letting the world around you squeeze you into its own mold." We have to stop chasing the fads offered by the world which everyone else is doing so that God's will can be done in our lives. If the masses are doing a particular thing, it's a pretty good indication that we do not need to get caught up in it. We have to guard against the propensity to do so.

The last responsibility we have to the will of God is that once it has been discovered, we must do it. To know and do the specific purpose for which we were created is the aim of life. God created us uniquely for a specific reason. God has planned work that he wants to do through us. This is another reason why knowing the will of God is so important. If that work is going to be done, we have to know God's will and do it. There is no greater way to honor God than to serve the purpose for which we were made.

God has a specific purpose for your life. It is the specific way that he wants you to fulfill his commission to make disciples. Have you discovered what it is? Have you found any of the clues that he has provided that you could make this discovery? You are encouraged to seek God's purpose until you find it. When you find it, live it every day of your life. Doing so will bring satisfaction to your life and pleasure to the God who created you as he did.

GOD'S SPECIFIC PURPOSE FOR THE BELIEVER'S LIFE
BLOCK 6 - THEME 5 - LESSON 2 (198 OF 216)
LESSON OUTLINE

I GOD HAS A SPECIFIC PLAN FOR YOUR LIFE
A. It is good
B. It is acceptable
C. It is perfect

II THREE RESPONSIBILITIES TOWARD GOD'S PLAN
A. Find out what it is
B. Overcome the obstacles to God's plan
C. Do it

SCRIPTURES TO BROADEN YOUR UNDERSTANDING
1. God has a purpose and work in mind for you
   Jeremiah 29:11
   Ephesians 2:10

2. People with a purpose
   Jeremiah - Jeremiah 1:5
   John the Baptist - John 1:19-23
   Peter - John 21:15-22
   Paul - Acts 9:6, 15-16
   Believers - Acts 1:8

LINES OF THEOLOGICAL CONNECTION
1. ANTHROPOLOGY
   The specific purpose of God for individual lives
   The desire of the heart
   The journey of desire

2. PNEUMATOLOGY
   Spiritual Gifts

3. ECCLESIOLOGY
   Our place in the body of Christ

GOD'S SPECIFIC PURPOSE FOR THE BELIEVER'S LIFE
BLOCK 6 - THEME 5 - LESSON 2 (198 OF 216)
QUESTIONS

1. What is God's general purpose for every believer?

2. What is the purpose of the specific purpose God has for each believer?

3. What clues has God given us to help us discover his specific purpose for our life?

4. What is the desire of your heart? (what you would really like to do with your life for God)

5. What is your spiritual gift?

6. How can you use your gift to create a disciple-making ministry for God?

7. Have you discovered your specific purpose?

8. Are you living each day according to God's specific purpose for your life?

19. ALMOST ANYTHING CAN BECOME A MINISTRY

THEME: GOD'S SPECIFIC PURPOSE

BLOCK 6 - THEME 5 - LESSON 3

LESSON AIM: Encourage disciples to look for a ministry in something they love to do.

SCRIPTURE: (Acts 6:1)

"And in those days, when the number of the disciples was multiplied, there arose a murmuring of the Grecians against the Hebrews, because their widows were neglected in the daily ministration."

The problem that took place in this verse of Scripture is one that is foreign to the church of today. In this episode of the early church, some Grecian ladies were overlooked and did not get to participate in the daily work of the ministry. So they complained. Today, we still have complaints, but they usually do not come from those who are left out of the work. Many Christians today are good with not having to work, but this was not true of the believers in the church at its beginning.

The term, "daily ministration" in the Greek language of the New Testament is the word from which we get the English word, deacon. It is a word which speaks of service, or ministry. In the context of verse one, it is used in reference to the ministry of the people of the church. The word is actually used three times in this passage with reference to three different groups of people. The other two groups are the pastors and the deacons of the church. Each group has ministry to do but with different priorities. Again, verse one has to do with the daily ministry of the people of the church.

As the title of this lesson states, almost anything at all can be turned into a ministry for the Lord. The word "almost" is inserted into the statement as a reminder that some things cannot become ministries. At times, an immature believer might suggest a ministry which is nothing less than participation in some kind of sin. So, we should remind ourselves that if something is specifically renounced in the Bible, we cannot expect to engage in that activity and call it a ministry. Therefore, we say that almost anything can become a ministry.

There are many ministries which are conducted daily in and through the local church and its members. These ministries are usually diverse enough for you to find a place to serve. However, the point is not simply to serve. The point is to try to find the service that God had in mind for you when he created you. God has chosen your place in the body of Christ and has determined specific works for you to do. He does not just want you to do something, but to do something specific. This specific thing is

91

the ministry you are looking for. These other ministries may be a place to get some training and experience but may not be the thing God wants you to do long term.

If you are seeking the ministry that God wants you to do, you can start your search with a simple three-step process. The first thing to do is a personal survey to try to identify your spiritual gift. When you were saved, you were indwelt by the Holy Spirit of God. The Holy Spirit gave you a spiritual gift which does two things. First, it equips you to do the service that God specifically wants you to do. God is so generous that he does not command us to work in a particular way without also providing the ability for us to do the work he commands. For example, if his intention is for us to teach, he gives us the spiritual gift of teaching so we can perform the ministry of teaching. Second, your spiritual gift is a clue to your specific ministry. A person with the gift of teaching obviously would do well in the ministry of teaching. If you think you have the gift of teaching, you can exercise that gift in some way to see how it feels for you. If it feels right, you build your main ministry around the work of teaching. This process works for any other ministry as well.

The next thing you should do in search of your specific ministry for the Lord is to try to discover the desire of your heart. This is a simple thing to say but not always a simple thing to do. The heart, as writer John Eldredge says, is the deepest, truest you. It is central to everything. Solomon said that God has set eternity in our heart and that out of it are the issues of life. Our adversary knows how important our heart is, much more than we do. The enemy begins from very early in our lives to destroy us on the level of the heart. If he can keep us from discovering our true identity and our true purpose, he can obstruct the work that God wants to accomplish through our life for his purposes. The adversary seeks very early to give us a wound in the heart. A wound like this can cripple us for life, robbing us of the abundant life God wants us to have. By the time most of us discover the truth about the heart, our heart has taken such a beating that we wonder if we have a heart at all. If we are ever to live the life of the heart, we have to uncover it from all the debris that has buried it, resuscitate it, and nurture it back to health so we can be and do what God wants for us.

God has set eternity in our hearts in our desire. God had a purpose in mind for us when he created us. He placed a desire in our heart which matches that purpose. The desire is another clue as to who we are, and to the ministry we are to do. At times, we get close to our desire without knowing what it is. These are the times when whatever we are doing feels like this is what we were made for. These are the moments we wish could last forever. Going back to these experiences in our lives can help us sort through all the distractions and help us uncover our desire. Asking ourselves what we really love to do is another way to discover our desire.

With the discovery of the clues God has given us, our spiritual gift, and the desire of our heart, we are then in a great position to develop a personal ministry for the Lord. The aim of all of our individual ministries is to make disciples of all nations. Knowing the aim of the ministry and knowing what we love to do and how we have been equipped to do it allows us to transform almost any common activity into a world-impacting ministry for Christ.

If you could do anything at all as a ministry for the Lord, what would you do? If there were no obstacles in your way; if you could make a particular thing into a ministry, what would it be? If an answer to these questions pops into your mind, you may be well on your way to discovering your personal ministry for Christ. Why don't you give it a try and see what happens? What do you have to lose?

ALMOST ANYTHING CAN BECOME A MINISTRY
BLOCK 6 - THEME 5 - LESSON 3 (199 OF 216)
LESSON OUTLINE

A simple process for beginning your personal ministry:

I DISCOVER YOUR SPIRITUAL GIFT
   A. Your gift equips you for your ministry
   B. Your gift is a clue to your ministry

II DISCOVER THE DESIRE OF YOUR HEART
   A. The heart is central to all
   B. Desire is a clue to your ministry

III DEVELOP YOUR PERSONAL MINISTRY
   A. The aim of ministry
   B. Let your clues guide you
   C. Give it a try

SCRIPTURES TO BROADEN YOUR UNDERSTANDING
1. The heart
   Proverbs 3:5-6
   Proverbs 4:23
   Ecclesiastes 3:11

2. Desire
   Psalms 37:3-5
   Ephesians 1:15-23

3. Personal ministry
   Ephesians 2:10; 4:1

4. Spiritual gifts
   Romans 12

LINES OF THEOLOGICAL CONNECTION
1. PNEUMATOLOGY
   Spiritual gifts

2. ANTHROPOLOGY
   Personal ministry
   The desire of the heart

3. ECCLESIOLOGY
   The great commission

ALMOST ANYTHING CAN BECOME A MINISTRY
BLOCK 6 - THEME 5 - LESSON 3 (199 OF 216)
QUESTIONS

1. List the three steps to a personal ministry.

2. What cannot be used as a personal ministry?

3. Have you discovered your spiritual gift?

4. Why is the heart important?

5. What clue has God placed within our heart?

6. Is there anything you would like to develop into a ministry for Christ?

7. How could you use your idea for a ministry to fulfill the great commission to make disciples?

8. What do you need to get your ministry idea off the ground?

20. TURN YOUR IDEA INTO A MINISTRY

THEME: GOD'S SPECIFIC PURPOSE

BLOCK 6 - THEME 5 - LESSON 4

LESSON AIM: Encourage disciples to try to turn their idea into a ministry.

SCRIPTURE: (2 Timothy 1:6)MSG

"And the special gift of ministry you received when I laid hands on you and prayed—keep that ablaze!"

There are a multitude of ministries in operation through the church today. And technology has made it possible to do ministry on such a large scale. Finding a ministry in which to be involved or starting a ministry today can be confusing to the believer who may be stepping out into this area for the first time. This lesson will offer some help in this direction.

There are basically two ways to start or get involved in a ministry. One way is to just jump in and become a part of something that is already going on, or to jump in and start a new work. If this just happens to be the thing God wants us to do, we will find along the way that God has given us what we need to be able to do the work. This is the way that most Christians start out in ministry, but it is a little like getting the cart before the horse, or like taking a gamble. We do not know if it will work out. Sometimes it can lead to discovering your specific purpose and ministry and can be a very good experience. Other times, it can be very frustrating. It is frustrating when we try to do something for which we are not equipped. When this happens, we are prone to give up or drop out most likely without ever finding a ministry that fits for us.

The other way to start or join a ministry is to think through it carefully before we begin. This takes longer but can lead to finding the right ministry for us without wasting a lot of time, resources, and effort.

The place to begin a new ministry is with an idea. We all have ideas all the time. Some of them are trivial and shallow; well-intended but will not necessarily accomplish what God wants us to accomplish. Other ideas are good ones, but still may not be what God has in mind. The best idea for a ministry comes in connection with our spiritual gift and the desire of our heart.

The problem is that the discovery of these three things does not always come in the same order for everybody. One may discover his gift first, while another may have an idea, and yet another will know his heart's desire. There is no rule which says these things must come in a particular order, but when they do come, they will have an obvious connection with each other. We begin the process of starting our ministry with whichever piece of the equation comes first. Then, we should look for the other two pieces. These three things are so important to know because they lead to a ministry built around the person rather than cramming a person into a ministry into which he does not fit. Ministry built around the person is the most natural and fulfilling kind. This is why Paul encouraged his young disciple, Timothy, to discover his spiritual gift and let it continuously motivate him into his ministry. This mode of operation still works for believers today. God has equipped us for a work. Knowing how he has equipped us can help us determine what the work is that we are to do.

When we know how our idea is connected to our spiritual gift and to the desire of our heart, we are ready to begin to develop our ministry. Let's say that you have an idea for the ministry you would like to do for the Lord. What is your next move? After the idea, your next move in ministry development is research. Ministry research includes several key areas of information which will help us get your ministry off to a good start and lead to success. To begin with, you want to have Biblical support for your ministry. You may have a theme verse that states what you want to accomplish with your work. There may be case studies in the Bible of those who have done a ministry similar to yours which you can study for help. There may be passages which give clear directions for a ministry such as yours. Let the Bible be your guide as you begin your ministry. And, of course, the ultimate Biblical goal is to fulfill the great commission. Write a statement about how your ministry will do this. A clear statement of how you intend to fulfill the great commission will go a long way in seeing that you get the job done.

Identify your target. Your target is the people to whom you will direct your ministry. Those people may be the homeless, the handicapped, abused children, single moms, young dads, families, senior adults, or unreached people groups. Your target may be a particular ethnic group, or within a certain country. Naturally, we want our ministries to impact as many people as possible, but they will be the most impactful when we focus on a specific target. This target must be identified from the start.

Good ideas often fail for lack of a plan to carry them out. Do not let this happen to you. Spend much time on your plan. The plan will include how you will organize and how you will do the work. Try to think through every detail of every scenario of your ministry. Decide on the best course of action by which to start and operate. Anticipate problems and have plans ready to implement should those problems be encountered. Be ready with your plan when it comes time to begin the work. And, expect the unexpected. There will be details that you missed; good ones and bad ones. When they surface, work through them, keeping your goal in mind. Do not let the unexpected derail your ministry. You must understand that your ministry is alive. Be prepared to make command decisions from the saddle.

Another important aspect of ministry is the people who will join you in the work. They fall into three general categories. Counselors are those people with whom we can share our dreams and plans, and who will give us sound Biblical advice or criticism. Their counsel can help us plan, protect, and perform the ministry we have in our heart. We may also need those people who will contribute financially or materially to our work. Some ministries serve as a link between those who have needs and those who have the means to meet those needs. Almost every ministry needs these people at some point along the way. And, we need those crew members who will actually do the work of the ministry. Depending on the mission and the scale of the mission, these people will vary from age, skill level, and education level. Regardless of the helpers we need, be they counselors, contributors, or crew members, our people have to be chosen, prepared and deployed with great care and responsibility on the part of the ministry and its leadership.

Having done your preparation in deciding what your ministry will do and researching how you will do it, you will be ready to launch your work for the Lord. Plans often look good on paper but turn out to be something else when put to work. As you begin your ministry, follow these four steps: try it, evaluate it, adjust it, and try it again. You may have to work through this cycle several times before you hit the stride of your ministry. Keep doing this until you know if it is going to work or not.

If God has given you an idea for ministry, he wants you to do it and to be successful. Stay with it. Do not give up on it. Do not quit. Get it done for his glory.

TURN YOUR IDEA INTO A MINISTRY
BLOCK 6 - THEME 5 - LESSON 4 (200 OF 216)
LESSON OUTLINE

Launching your ministry:

I WHAT IS YOUR IDEA?
   A. Clue - spiritual gift
   B. Clue - desire of the heart

II DO YOUR RESEARCH
   A. Biblical support
   B. Your target
   C. Your plan
   D. Your helpers

III LAUNCH YOUR MINISTRY
   A. Try it
   B. Evaluate it
   C. Adjust it
   D. Try it again

SCRIPTURES TO BROADEN YOUR UNDERSTANDING
1. Your ministry is important
   1 Corinthians 12:18
   1 Corinthians 15:58

2. Stay with your ministry
   Romans 11:29
   1 Timothy 6:20
   2 Timothy 1:14

3. Dream big for your ministry
   Ephesians 3:20-21

LINES OF THEOLOGICAL CONNECTION
1. ANTHROPOLOGY
   Developing your personal ministry
   Talents
   Acquired Skills

2. ECCLESIOLOGY
   Ministry in and through the church

3. PNEUMATOLOGY
   Empowerment for ministry through the Holy Spirit
   Spiritual gifts

TURN YOUR IDEA INTO A MINISTRY
BLOCK 6 - THEME 5 - LESSON 4 (200 OF 216)
QUESTIONS

1. What are the three steps to help you start a ministry for the Lord.

2. What kind of help can we get for our ministry from the Bible?

3. What things should be included in our research for a personal ministry?

4. Who are among the helpers we need for our ministry?

5. List the four-part cycle that helps us get our ministry running properly.

6. Do you have an idea for a personal ministry? What is it?

7. With whom can you talk that can help you develop your ministry idea?

8. Are you willing to step out and give your ministry idea a try?

21. READING THE BIBLE

THEME: YOUR DEVOTIONAL LIFE

BLOCK 6 - THEME 6 - LESSON 1

LESSON AIM: Share the importance and benefit from reading God's Word.

SCRIPTURE: (Deuteronomy 17:18-20)

18 And it shall be, when he sitteth upon the throne of his kingdom, that he shall write him a copy of this law in a book out of that which is before the priests the Levites: 19 And it shall be with him, and he shall read therein all the days of his life: that he may learn to fear the LORD his God, to keep all the words of this law and these statutes, to do them: 20 That his heart be not lifted up above his brethren, and that he turn not aside from the commandment, to the right hand, or to the left: to the end that he may prolong his days in his kingdom, he, and his children, in the midst of Israel.

God has a purpose for our individual lives on the earth. Before he made the world, God knew us and had a purpose in mind just for us. He gave us the Word of God to help us discover his purpose for our life and to guide us in the fulfillment of his purpose. The Word of God is irreplaceable in our life as a believer in Christ Jesus. If we are to know God's purpose and do it, we must be a reader of the Scriptures on a regular basis to develop and continue the work God has planned for us to do.

Speaking to the children of Israel concerning a part of his plan for them, God said that he would give them a king according to his choosing. If the king would be blessed and serve faithfully before God, he would have to read the Words of God, keeping them ever before himself. There would be everlasting benefit which would come from simply reading the Word of God. We can have the same benefits in our lives if we will read it as well.

In this passage, we see something of the discipline of reading. While there are some people who seemingly live to read, for others, reading is something that they have to make themselves do. It takes time to read, and reading is work. It requires concentration and thinking to be able to comprehend the text and try to understand the writer's intent in writing. For those who find it difficult to engage in the work of reading, bright sunny days many times win out over the time and effort it takes to read a book of any kind, and especially the Bible.

God said the king of Israel would have to be a reader. The king was to have a book containing the laws of the Lord, and he was to read it. As he read it, two things would occur. First, he would learn to fear the Lord God. As he read God's words, he would understand many things about God. He would learn who God is and that there is none other like him. He would learn that God was to be approached in a specified way. He would learn that God had given laws to man to show him how to live his life on earth in a way that would be pleasing to the God who created him. He would learn that there are things in this world that should be avoided and the reasons for avoiding them. He would learn of the opportunity to live his life in a way that would go on making impact for God many years after the king's death. All these things and much more the king would know if he would only read God's Word. The second thing that would happen is that in reading the Word, and knowing what God required, the king would be able to do those things that God wanted. He would learn to fear the Lord, or to have respect for the things God required, and he would be able to do those very things.

The same things are before us when we make reading the Word of God an important part of our life. We learn what God wants so we can do what God wants. If we do not read the Word, we cannot know the things God requires of us. God wants to lead us but he leads us according to his Word. Therefore we have to read it in order to govern our life by the ways of the Lord.

God made it clear to the king that if he would read his words, he would reap several benefits from his reading. To begin with, reading the word of God would combat the pride of the sinful nature of man. Pride is often referred to as the original sin. It was found in the heart of Lucifer which led to an attempt to overthrow God's rule over his creation. It was used against Adam and Eve in the Garden of Eden. It is perhaps the chief weapon of the adversary in his arsenal against the believer in Christ. Man constantly battles with pride. The thing about pride is that it often cleverly disguises itself in a false humility, making it difficult to detect. Pride goes before our destructions. God hates it and avoids those who have it in their life. Reading the Word of God is a deterrent to the awful sin of pride and its destruction.

Reading the Word of God would also keep the king upon the path God wanted him to follow. It would provide balance for him as he sought to live right before the Lord. The Word of God would keep him from going too far to the left or to the right from the path revealed in God's Word. There has to be a balance in life. It is not that life is always either black or white. Neither is it that there is the gray area of compromising the truth. The thing is that there is grace and mercy where sin abounds and a person who is too far to the right or left of God's Word will never be able to respond to others, or to himself, in grace and mercy. It is the Word of God and the regular reading of it which helps a man stay on God's path of life.

Another benefit the king would have by reading God's Word was that the time of his work would be prolonged. He could have a long-lasting rule on earth if he would walk in the ways of the Lord. We may recall King Saul, Israel's very first king. In the very first assignment God gave him, Saul disobeyed God's Word and lost the kingdom. He ruled another forty years before the kingdom was taken from him but they were years of intense internal turmoil as Saul distrusted even the closest and most loyal people around him. Walking in the ways of the Lord revealed as we read God's Word produces longevity in our service for the Lord. We have a wonderful example of this in our own time in the life of Billy Graham. It is said that he and his ministry partners agreed at the beginning of the ministry together to walk in the ways of the Lord. Consequently, Mr. Graham's ministry continues today in his 97th year of life. His ministry is one of the most impactful, far-reaching, and above reproach ministries in history.

A fourth benefit God named to the king that he would have if he read and kept the Word of God is that his work and influence would continue in the world through his offspring. The Word of God has the ability to do this because the Bible reveals God's strategy of spiritual reproduction. Throughout the Word of God, we find examples of those who taught faithful men and women who were able to teach others also. This is the primary means of spreading the gospel of Christ and the ways of the Lord throughout the whole earth. Believers in Christ are to learn this strategy and practice it during their life on earth. The span of life becomes immaterial when we learn how to reproduce disciples of Christ. Reproduce even one reproducing disciple and your life will go on making an impact for God after you leave this world.

These are great benefits which are available to anyone who will take the time and the trouble to make reading the Word of God a regular part of his life. Make it your goal to read through the Bible again and again. Doing so will reap a great harvest.

READING THE BIBLE
BLOCK 6 - THEME 6 - LESSON 1 (201 OF 216)
LESSON OUTLINE

I THE DISCIPLINE OF READING
    A. Learn to fear the Lord
    B. Keep the law of God

II THE BENEFITS OF READING
    A. Combat pride in the heart
    B. Stay on God's pathway
    C. Prolong your work on earth
    D. Continue through offspring

SCRIPTURES TO BROADEN YOUR UNDERSTANDING
1. Reading the Word of God
    Exodus 24:7
    Joshua 8:34
    2 Kings 23
    Nehemiah 8-9
    Luke 4:16
    Acts 8:30
    Acts 13:15
    Colossians 4:16
    1 Thessalonians 5:27

LINES OF THEOLOGICAL CONNECTION
1. THE DOCTRINE OF THE SCRIPTURES
   Reading the Bible
   Bible translations
   Using reading guides

2. DISCIPLE-MAKING
   Reproduction and multiplication strategy
   Everlasting life

3. THE DOCTRINE OF SATAN
   His use and misuse of the word of God
   The doctrine of demons

4. PNEUMATOLOGY
   The Spirit illuminates as we read the Word of God

READING THE BIBLE
BLOCK 6 - THEME 6 - LESSON 1 (201 OF 216)
QUESTIONS

1. Why should we read the Word of God?

2. List four benefits from reading the Word of God.

3. Is Bible reading a part of your regular routine?

4. Have you ever read the Bible all the way through?

5. Why should you read the Bible again and again?

6. Share some way or ways that your Bible reading has helped you in your life.

7. What difficulty do you find in reading the Bible?

8. Who can you encourage to begin reading the Bible?

22. BIBLE STUDY TOOLS

THEME: YOUR DEVOTIONAL LIFE

BLOCK 6 - THEME 6 - LESSON 2

LESSON AIM: Build your Bible study library with a few helpful tools.

SCRIPTURE: (2 Timothy 2:15)

Study to shew thyself approved unto God, a workman that needeth not to be ashamed, rightly dividing the word of truth.

Believe it or not every Christian is a theologian. Theology is the study of God, and a theologian is one who studies God. Charles Ryrie wrote that there is nothing wrong with being an amateur theologian, but there is everything wrong with being a sloppy theologian. There is no excuse for being a sloppy theologian today when there are so many tools available to help us in our study of the Word of God. We should be the best theologians we can possibly be, reading, studying, understanding, applying and communicating God's Word.

Every Christian should have a library of some sort to aid in the study of the Bible. Of course, libraries will vary from person to person. Some may have a great love for books and will collect many of them over the years. Others may not have the time, resources, space, or the inclination to have a great number of books on hand. It is not the size of the library that matters but the content and use of it that helps us get the most from our Bible study.

Regardless of the size of your library, there are a few essential tools that every student of the Bible should have. Following is a list of the essentials. You are encouraged to begin to build your Bible study library by collecting these tools and learning to use them.

1. BIBLES

Every library should contain at least three copies of the Bible. One is the King James Version simply because it is one of the oldest and most often used English versions of the Bible. Many other books refer to the KJV so it just makes good sense to have one. Bible students should also have a translation that is easy to read. The KJV is not always easy for some people to read and understand. Get yourself an English version that is easy to read. It does not help to read a version that you do not understand. This will frustrate you and cause you to stop reading the Bible. Finally, it is good to have a good study Bible to help you connect all the many pieces of the Bible puzzle.

107

2. SURVEYS

Every library needs at least one copy each of an Old Testament Survey and a New Testament Survey. Surveys provide background information on each book of the Bible. They usually include historical background on each book, the writer of the book, where and when the book was written, and the audience to whom the book was written. They provide an outline of the book and other pertinent information to help in getting the message of the book.

3. BIBLE ENCYCLOPEDIA

Bible encyclopedias come in sets from small to large numbers of volumes. They are like any other encyclopedia except their information is related to the things found in the Bible. They are arranged from A to Z. Choose a set of encyclopedias which have good content, easy to read and follow, and with the number of volumes for which you have the space.

4. BIBLE DICTIONARY

A Bible dictionary contains much of the same information as an encyclopedia but in more concise form. They contain information on people, places, Bible books and so forth. This will be one of your most used Bible study tools.

5. STRONG'S CONCORDANCE

The Strong's Concordance contains every word in the Bible numbered to a Hebrew and Greek dictionary of words. They provide the Scripture reference of every word, the word in the original language with its spelling and definitions. This helps in interpreting and understanding the Bible.

6. THEOLOGY REFERENCE BOOK

The Bible is not arranged in order by its subjects. Pieces of each doctrine are scattered here and there throughout the Bible. This is part of the difficulty in reading and understanding the Bible. A theology reference book helps to put all the pieces that go together in the same box so the student can get a grasp of each theological subject.

7. WORD STUDY BOOKS

It has been said that a picture is worth a thousand words. The student of the Bible also knows that a word is sometimes worth a thousand pictures. The words of the Bible provide pictures of the messages contained within them. Word study books in Greek and Hebrew are essential to knowing the message of the Bible and communicating it clearly and colorfully.

8. BIBLE ATLAS

The Bible names many places. Some of the names of the cities are still in use today. Others are lost in antiquity. When reading a Bible passage, it sometimes helps to look at the atlas to see where the events took place. Tracing the routes of people in the Bible stories also helps by use of the Bible atlas.

9. COMMENTARIES

Many commentaries exist on every book of the Bible. Some of them can be trusted, some cannot. The works of some commentators are considered essential. It takes time and effort to get to know which ones you can trust. Learn to read the Bible first and listen to what God says to you before you run to a commentary. The commentary is useful when checking your thoughts with other students of the Bible. They also provide information on the text that aids in understanding it.

10. EXPLORE THE BOOK - by J. Sidlow Baxter

While I do not endorse every point of view held by Mr. Baxter, his work is found to be an essential work on understanding the structure and story of the Bible.

These works are a few essentials every student of the Bible needs in his Bible study library. Put them on your birthday and Christmas wish lists. You can also find these and many other works on computer software programs or online. Take advantage of the ones which work for you and of where you may access them. Learn to use them as you study the Word of God. With all the help that is available, there is no reason why any one cannot become a great theologian and student of the Word of God.

BIBLE STUDY TOOLS
BLOCK 6 - THEME 6 - LESSON 2 (202 OF 216): BIBLE STUDY TOOLS
QUESTIONS

1. Do you presently own any of the books listed in this lesson?

2. Have you discovered where you can have access to these reference tools such as online or in your church library?

3. Do you make regular use of these tools in your study of the Bible?

4. What are your favorite Bible Study tools?

23. MEMORIZING SCRIPTURE

THEME: YOUR DEVOTIONAL LIFE

BLOCK 6 - THEME 6 - LESSON 3

LESSON AIM: Share important reasons to memorize Scripture.

SCRIPTURE: (Psalm 119:11)

Thy word have I hid in mine heart, that I might not sin against thee.

Culture today is counter to memorization. Everything is built to relieve man of this responsibility. We have smart televisions and smart telephones which almost do the thinking for us. We certainly do not have to memorize telephone numbers any more. They are in storage in our phones and all we have to do is select the correct menu where we can find them. With the press of a button, or even by asking our phone to dial the number for us, our calls are made.

Time was when everything had to be committed to memory. We memorized phone numbers, birthdates, and anniversaries. School children had to memorize the multiplication tables, at least through the number twelve. Now, many of us may only know a small handful of phone numbers. Memorization has nearly become a lost art in our own lifetime.

One area which still pays off in rich dividends is in the area of Scripture memory. While we have gotten away from this blessing and discipline in the church of today, its rewards are no less beneficial. Many of us memorized Bible verses as children in Sunday School that are still in our hearts today. We can recall chapter and verse as well as the text and quote them just as we learned them years ago. They will be with us as long as God allows us to have a sound mind in this world.

Scripture memory affords many blessings to the person who practices it. Let's talk about three of these blessings. First, Scripture memory makes it possible for us to meditate in God's Word. It is a wonderful thing to have a copy of the Bible in our own language. This is a blessing that not every person on earth has to enjoy. We love to read the Bible and spend time with God, centered around his Word. However, there are times when we are busy going about the everyday business of life when we cannot carry an open Bible with us, reading it and pouring over its content. But, if we have memorized Scripture, we can call up the verses we have memorized and dwell on them no matter what else we may be doing. We can be busy with our hands in one area and at the same time, meditate on God's word.

Meditating on the Word is not to assume a trance-like position or mode, seeking to distance ourselves from reality. It is to think on the Word and digest it in our hearts so that we can live it in our lives. Meditation may be done to help us relate Scripture with Scripture. As we think on one verse, we may be reminded of a similar verse in another place and a connection is made in our minds with these Scripture references. This broadens our command of the Scriptures when we are able to see these important connections. We may meditate also to help us understand a verse or verse portion which has been unclear to us in the past. By thinking on it, dwelling on it, pondering over it, looking at it from every angle, we can begin to understand the truth contained in the verse. Meditation, therefore, helps us get to the truth which may be hidden to the natural eye. Meditation also helps us in the self-examination of our lives. As we think on the truth, at the same time, we can look at our own life to see if we measure up to the truth or not. Meditating on the Word reveals the discrepancies in our lives, giving us the opportunity to correct the things that do not align with the Word of God.

Next, memorizing Scripture creates a guard in our hearts against sin. David, in the theme verse for this lesson, said that he memorized God's Word so that he might not sin against God. As we read the Scriptures, we come across those things in life that please God and those things which are displeasing to him. The natural propensity of man, of course, is to do those things which are displeasing to God. If we have memorized Scriptures which tell us to not do something, when we are tempted to do those things, we may recall the Scripture which told us to avoid that thing. The Scripture becomes a guard for us, warning us that we are about to step into an area with which God is not pleased. If we listen to the guard of Scripture, we can avoid the sin and do the right thing in the eyes of God. Conversely, when we have memorized Scriptures which speak of things which are pleasing to God, we can know that when we follow the exhortation of those verses hidden in our heart, God is pleased with our actions and with our obedience to his Word.

A third benefit of Scripture memorization has to do with the spiritual warfare in which the believer is engaged on a daily basis. We have an adversary which walks about as a roaring lion seeking whom he may devour. A person who has hidden the Word of God in his heart is not an easy person to devour. This is one who can put up a fight with the enemy and prevail through the use of the sword of the Spirit which is the word of God. When we memorize Scripture, we are building a magazine of spiritual munitions in our heart from which the Holy Spirit can draw when we encounter the enemy. The Holy Spirit will call up just the right Scripture from our memory to help us in the time of need. Jesus demonstrated this in the wilderness during the time of his temptation. With every attack and temptation from the devil, Jesus responded by saying, "It is written...", then he proceeded to quote a verse of Scripture that met and won over the temptation of the moment. The Word of God will work in the same way for us if we will hide it in our heart, making it ready for the time of need.

The final benefit we will mention about Scripture memory is that it aids us in witnessing for the Lord Jesus Christ. We never know when God is going to drop us in the middle of an opportunity to share the gospel. We can be prepared for this by memorizing Scriptures about salvation. There are many passages which speak to the need of the heart of man and what God has done through Jesus to meet that need. We should hide these Scriptures in our heart to be ready when the Holy Spirit opens the door for us to witness. From the Word we have memorized, God can use us to lead a person to faith in Jesus Christ. There are also those times when we have opportunity to respond to the questions people are asking about life and the things they are experiencing. We can be ready with the answers by memorizing Scriptures which speak to the different needs and experiences we all encounter in life. When a question is presented to us, we can ask God to give us the answer we need to give to them by helping us recall just the right verse we have memorized from the Word of God. Solomon said there is nothing like being able to share just the right words to him that is weary.

The Word of God is one of the most important things we have in order to get through life in this world. The other top two things are the Holy Spirit and prayer, but even they work in conjunction with the Word of God. Scripture memory is a great benefit we have for living. It takes a little work to do it, but it pays off in blessings which are to be had in no other way. Do not sell yourself short on these blessings by failing to hide the Word of God in your heart.

MEMORIZING SCRIPTURE
BLOCK 6 - THEME 6 - LESSON 3 (203 OF 216)
LESSON OUTLINE

Benefits of Scripture Memory:

I MEDITATION
   A. Helps us connect Scripture with Scripture
   B. Helps us understand the truth
   C. Aids in self-examination

II GUARDS OUR HEART
   A. Things not to do
   B. Things to do

III SPIRITUAL WARFARE
   A. The enemy attacks
   B. The Holy Spirit counter-attacks with the Word of God

IV WITNESSING
   A. Sharing the gospel
   B. Answering questions

SCRIPTURES TO BROADEN YOUR UNDERSTANDING
1. Take a concordance and look up the Scripture references to meditation.

LINES OF THEOLOGICAL CONNECTION
1. THE DOCTRINE OF THE SCRIPTURES
   Memorizing the Word of God
   Meditating on the Word of God

2. PNEUMATOLOGY
   The work of the Spirit through the Scriptures in our memory

3. THE DOCTRINE OF SATAN
   Satan has no defense against the Word of God

4. ANTHROPOLOGY
   Be prepared to defend your faith with the Word of God
   Be prepared to extend the faith with the Word of God

MEMORIZING SCRIPTURE
BLOCK 6 - THEME 6 - LESSON 3 (203 OF 216)
QUESTIONS

1. List four benefits of memorizing Scripture.

2. What benefit do we get from meditating on the Word of God?

3. How can the Holy Spirit help us either in spiritual warfare or in a witnessing opportunity?

4. Share a time when the Holy Spirit gave you a verse to use in a time of need.

5. Is Scripture memory a part of your spiritual disciplines?

6. What important verses do you need to hide in your heart beginning today?

24. PRAYER

THEME: YOUR DEVOTIONAL LIFE

BLOCK 6 - THEME 6 - LESSON 4

LESSON AIM: Learn to pray as Jesus taught his followers to pray

SCRIPTURE: (Matthew 6:9-13)

⁹ After this manner therefore pray ye: Our Father which art in heaven, Hallowed be thy name. ¹⁰ Thy kingdom come. Thy will be done in earth, as it is in heaven. ¹¹ Give us this day our daily bread. ¹² And forgive us our debts, as we forgive our debtors. ¹³ And lead us not into temptation, but deliver us from evil: For thine is the kingdom, and the power, and the glory, forever. Amen.

Prayer is a spiritual discipline in which every believer should engage on a regular basis. It is one part of the two-part means of communion we have with God: the Word of God and prayer. When we read the Word, God speaks to us; when we pray, we speak to God. And, God many times also speaks to us as we pray. In the model prayer in Jesus' Sermon on the Mount, he gave us a guide to our praying. If we will follow this guide, we will cover all the bases when we pray.

In the model prayer, Jesus taught us to pray with three views in mind. The first thing to do in prayer is to look up when we pray. Many times, in prayer, we rush in to God's presence with our list of needs and wants, forgetting to spend some time reminding ourselves that we are speaking to the God of the universe and recognizing him as such. Jesus taught us to take a moment to acknowledge him and his holiness as he governs the universe from his throne in heaven. This will give us an opportunity to worship him as he deserves to be worshipped. And, it will remind us of our relationship with him and with our brothers and sisters in Christ. He is our Father, and we are part of a family. This in itself goes a long way in helping us have a better perspective on the things we are about to present to him in prayer. Knowing that we have a father and a family reminds us that we are not alone in the world and that someone cares about us and about our needs. We need to look up when we pray.

Second, we are to look around when we pray. In this passage, verses 10-13 give us four topics to include in our prayers as we look around in the world on any given day. First, we are to align ourselves with God's plans. How many times do we rush to God to try to convince him to adjust everything in the world to fit our agenda instead of his? Jesus taught us to remember the larger story of God's purpose by praying, "Thy kingdom come". In other words, we are to align with God's purpose, not the other way around. Next, he said, "Thy will be done in earth as it is in heaven." This is another way to say that the smaller stories of our lives are to be aligned and adjusted to the larger story of God's purpose in the world. So, prayer is an opportunity to be reminded of that which is most important and that we are to calibrate our life to what God is up to in the world.

Jesus taught us to pray next with an awareness of the true source of our provisions, and he is that source. So many times we depend upon our employer and the pay check that we receive from them as our source of provision. While they are used by God to provide for us, God is the true source of our provision. We are to be reminded in prayer that this is true. The daily provision illustrated by the bread comes to us ultimately from God. It is our Father who feeds us and clothes us and shelters us and provides for us in every way. This perspective makes us more grateful and thankful for what God does for us every day, and it makes us aware of how much God is directly involved in our daily lives.

Jesus included in his model prayer an admonition concerning our relationships. The first relationship he mentioned is our relationship with God. This is found in the phrase, "forgive us", in verse twelve. When we pray, we have to make sure there is nothing to hinder our fellowship with God. Sin in our life is a good way to keep our prayers from being answered. We have to make sure that we keep everything out in the open and confessed before God. He knows all these things anyway, so it is for our benefit, not his. Next, Jesus brings our relationships with others into view. We are to ask God to forgive us, "as we forgive others". We are to practice forgiveness to the same degree that we receive it. If we are unwilling to forgive another person, we come to God with sin in our life which hinders our prayers. In order for our relationship with God to be all it can be, our relationships with others have to be right as well. We may be able to put a mask on a bad relationship with someone but prayer is the one place where all the masks come off and we stand before God as we are. God has so rigged prayer that we cannot hide unforgiveness in our heart toward another person when we come to him in prayer.

Another important topic Jesus mentioned in prayer is the arena of spiritual warfare. There is a war going on and the believer cannot escape it. It takes place on two battle fronts of which we must be aware. The first battlefront is the war within each one of us. This is addressed in the phrase, "lead us not into temptation". This is the war on the inside of every person which takes place between the spirit and the flesh; between the old man and the new man; between sin and righteousness. This battle primarily is fought on the battlefield of our mind. It is waged through the thoughts which bombard our minds constantly each day and night. With a single thought, the adversary can build a stronghold in our life from which they can fuel the war within. Paul exhorted us to bring every thought under to obedience and control of Jesus Christ. To arrest every thought that we have speaks of the intensity of the warfare and the vigilance required to carry on the fight.

The other battlefront on which the believer must fight is war that takes place on the outside, the evil about us from which we need to be delivered. Evil is in the world. It is found all over the world in people like terrorists who take the lives of innocent people in horrific ways. It is also found down the street and around the corner from every one of us in those who are led to do the evil works of Satan against mankind. Evil is even closer to home than this as it can come from our own old nature if we allow ourselves to live in the flesh. Part of our praying should include asking God to help us when we are confronted with evil in the world and to make sure that we are not a channel through which evil can come to others.

Jesus taught us to look up and look around when we pray. Finally, he taught us to look ahead in prayer as well. He taught us to keep an eye toward the future coming kingdom of the Lord Jesus Christ. One day, Jesus is coming to the earth and will rule the entire world for one thousand years. Beyond this millennial kingdom is the glorious eternity he has prepared for those who believe in him. We are to think on these things and pray, looking forward in their direction to the time when these wonderful things will come to pass.

When you pray, look up, look around, and look ahead. When we look up and look ahead, we are in a better spiritual condition to deal with life as we look around at all the things we have to experience and endure in this life. Practice the discipline of prayer, learning to pray as Jesus taught from these three perspectives.

PRAYER
BLOCK 6 - THEME 6 - LESSON 4 (204 OF 216)
LESSON OUTLINE

When you pray:

I LOOK UP (v9)
A. Acknowledge God in prayer
Our Father which art in heaven, hallowed be thy name
1. Father
2. Family - Our

II LOOK AROUND (V10-13a)
A. Align with God's plans (v10)
1. The larger story - thy kingdom come
2. The smaller story - thy will be done in earth as in heaven
B. Awareness of the true source of provisions (v11)
1. Source - Give (God)
2. Sharing - Us
3. Sustenance - Bread
4. Schedule - Daily
C. Admonition concerning relationships (v12)
1. Relationship with God - Forgive us
2. Relationship with others - As we forgive others
D. Arena of spiritual warfare (v13a)
1. The war within - Lead us not into temptation
2. The war without - But deliver us from evil

III LOOK AHEAD (v13b)
A. Assume an apocalyptic posture in prayer
Thine is the kingdom, and the power, and the glory forever

SCRIPTURES TO BROADEN YOUR UNDERSTANDING
1. Use your concordance to look up references to prayer in the Scriptures.

LINES OF THEOLOGICAL CONNECTION
1. THE DOCTRINE OF PRAYER
   Practice prayer
   Pray continually
   How to pray

2. THE DOCTRINE OF GOD
   God works through our prayers

PRAYER
BLOCK 6 - THEME 6 - LESSON 4 (204 OF 216)
QUESTIONS

1. What are the three simple perspectives from which Jesus taught us to pray?

2. What is the first thing we should do in prayer?

3. What things did Jesus teach us to include in our prayers when we look around?

4. What are the two battlefields on which a believer must wage spiritual warfare?

5. Where is the battle fought on the inside?

6. How do we commune with God?

7. Is prayer a part of your daily discipline?

25. THE MANDATE

THEME: DISCIPLE-MAKING

BLOCK 6 - THEME 7 - LESSON 1

LESSON AIM: Jesus commanded every believer to make disciples.

SCRIPTURE: (Matthew 28:18-20)

18 And Jesus came and spake unto them, saying, All power is given unto me in heaven and in earth. 19 Go ye therefore, and teach all nations, baptizing them in the name of the Father, and of the Son, and of the Holy Ghost: 20 Teaching them to observe all things whatsoever I have commanded you: and, lo, I am with you alway, even unto the end of the world. Amen.

Between his resurrection and ascension, Jesus gave the mandate of world conquest to his followers. We call it the great commission. He offered them the world on God's terms. They accepted those terms and made a lasting spiritual impact on the world. The genius of his strategy was simply this: while you are going about your daily business, make disciples. Not just converts, but fully devoted reproducing followers of Christ. Jesus did not encumber them, or us, with extra duties to add to their busy schedules. He said to them, "You have to be out in the world anyway in the course of your daily lives. Let this objective of making disciples for world impact be the main objective of all that you do. Recruit and make disciples wherever you are at any given time. Make disciples while you work. Make disciples while you play. Let this be the focus of all that you do all the time, and I will give you the world! And, by the way, while you are doing it, I will be with you every step of the way."

The same mandate holds true for believers in Christ in the twenty-first century. God has not changed his mind or his purpose. The job is not yet complete. Until it is, we all have the assignment of fulfilling the commission to make disciples. This is true of every believer regardless of age. We are commanded to do this work. God has given us everything necessary to do the job.

The first thing God has given us to fulfill his commission is power in which to work. "All power is given unto me in heaven and in earth", Jesus said. The word for power that he used is *exousia*. It means authority. Jesus has all authority in every realm that concerns man: heaven and earth; the here and the hereafter. He is God with divine authority in time and eternity. He is the only one worthy of such authority that was given by the heavenly Father. Therefore, he is able to say, "Whatever you do in my name, according to my will, you will be endorsed and supported by the very throne of God. Whatever you do will have my fingerprints on it, because I, living in you, will extend my life through you." His power through his presence in us is what we have through which to work.

In addition to his power, Jesus also gave us a process to use whereby we can fulfill his commission. Just as Jesus was given his power, or authority, by the Father, he wants to send his reproducing followers throughout the world, sanctioned by this same authority. This authority, however, is only available to those who are following and fulfilling the process of building more reproducing, world-impacting disciples in the same way that Jesus built them. His command is to make disciples as you are going by enlisting them into the process of learning to obey his teachings. The process, according to this passage, is to evangelize, baptize, and train believers in the purpose and plan of God.

The church of today has only partially fulfilled this process. We have done a good job of evangelism and baptizing, although even these are in decline now. But where we have done an insufficient job is in the area of making disciples, which is the most important thing we are to do. This is the reason we have so many ineffective and inconsistent Christians in our churches today. It is also the direct cause of the decline of the church in America in our day. Evangelism is important but it is not an end in itself. It is merely one step in a larger process. To focus on any step to the exclusion of the others is to weaken the process and diminish the results that God wants us to have. If we will evangelize with a goal to turn the evangelized into world-impacting disciples, we will fulfill this process with the full authority of the Lord Jesus Christ.

When we go in Christ's authority, working according to his process and obeying his mandate to build disciples, we receive a special promise from God. Jesus said, "As you do this, I will be with you." We are not alone as we move out into a dark, lost world. We are on a co-mission: a mission with Jesus Christ. As long as we follow Christ's instructions, we will enjoy his presence with us to the ends of the earth until the end of time.

Many promises in the Bible are often linked to a process of some kind. This promise is linked to the process of building disciples. The context of this passage is not about Christ's presence with us in salvation. We know that once God comes into our spirit, he never leaves or forsakes us. We are saved eternally. Rather, this promise has to do with his purpose for us in service to him. According to this passage, if we are not reproducing disciples for world-impact, we need not expect Christ to be around us very long. He will be with those who are obedient to his Word. His eyes run to and fro throughout the whole earth to show himself strong on behalf of those whose heart is perfect toward him. This explains why the manifested presence and power of God are missing in many churches and in the lives of many believers. In relation to the great commission, it is only those followers of Christ who are fulfilling God's mandate to make disciples who will experience the presence of God in their midst on a regular basis. These are the believers who can legitimately claim the promise of the presence of Christ with them as they go.

You can have a strategic impact in the world for Christ. The thing you must decide is which offer of the world will you choose? God is offering you the world. Satan is also offering you the world. God's offer of the world is eternal. Satan's offer is temporary. God's offer may involve grief now but glory later. Satan's offer involves glory now and grief later. In a strange way, the grief of God's offer is a privilege instead of a burden. By the same token, the present glory of Satan's offer still leaves us unsatisfied and empty. Jesus expressed this truth by asking, "What does it profit a man to gain the whole world (Satan's offer) and lose his eternal soul in the process?

You are accepting one of those offers each day. Be careful, though. You may not always recognize Satan's offer. He is a master of disguise. Most people would not openly bow to Satan in organized worship, but they still serve him nonetheless. They can accept his offer of the world without realizing it. They simply mind their own business with little concern for the lost or for God's offer of the world as he wants it to be. We reach for our dreams, our piece of the pie in the sky. We are content with a comfortable house, a nice family, our pets, jobs, or careers and all the things we do to entertain ourselves. There is no greater example of someone who has accepted Satan's offer of the world than the comfortable, prospering Christian who goes to church every Sunday but never reproduces one disciple in obedience to the command of Jesus Christ to do so.

On the other hand, God offers the world to us also. He says "Ask of me, and I shall give thee the heathen for thine inheritance, and the uttermost parts of the earth for thy possession." The world he offers is a share in what he is doing among the family of mankind. His offer is extended, but few Christians accept it. To accept God's offer is to accept his terms of the offer as well. The terms are: believe in Christ, obey the great commission, and give your life for this purpose. The benefits are an impact in the world now, a life that goes on making an impact after your death, and a never-ending life with God for eternity to come. There is no greater offer of the world in the world than this.

God has mandated, or commanded, that his followers reproduce reproducing disciples of all peoples of the world. You may do a lot of things in this world during your lifetime, but if you do not do this, you will have missed the purpose of your being on this earth in the first place. Which offer of the world will you accept?

THE MANDATE
BLOCK 6 - THEME 7 - LESSON 1 (205 OF 216)
LESSON OUTLINE

I THE POWER FOR THE COMMISSION
A. Authority
B. Support

II THE PROCESS FOR THE COMMISSION
A. Evangelize
B. Baptize
C. Train

III THE PROMISE FOR THE COMMISSION
A. The presence of Christ
B. Linked to a process

IV TWO OFFERS OF THE WORLD
A. On God's terms
B. On Satan's terms

SCRIPTURES TO BROADEN YOUR UNDERSTANDING
1. The great commission
   Gen 1:28
   Matthew 28:18-20
   Mark 16:15-18
   Luke 24:46-49
   Acts 1:8
2. Make disciples
   2 Timothy 2:2

3. Jesus' strategic process for mentoring
   John 17

LINES OF THEOLOGICAL CONNECTION
1. THE DOCTRINE OF DISCIPLE-MAKING
   The commission is to all believers
   Evangelism

2. ECCLESIOLOGY
   The church ordinances

3. THE DOCTRINE OF SATAN
   Satan's goal for the believer
   Satanic disguise

4. ANTHROPOLOGY
   The lure of the world

THE MANDATE
BLOCK 6 - THEME 7 - LESSON 1 (205 OF 216)
QUESTIONS

1. What is the basic command of the great commission?

2. What is the difference between evangelism and disciple-making?

3. Where can disciple-making be done?

4. Why is evangelism not an end in itself?

5. Who is to do the work of evangelism?

6. Who is to do the work of disciple-making?

7. Is God's purpose any different today from that of the believers in the first century?

8. List the three steps in the disciple-making process from Matthew 28.

Allen L. Elder

26. THE METHOD

THEME: DISCIPLE-MAKING

BLOCK 6 - THEME 7 - LESSON 2

LESSON AIM: Look at the disciple-making method of Jesus from a different angle.

SCRIPTURE: (2 Timothy 1:9-10)PT

"For he has rescued us from all that is really evil and called us to a life of holiness - not because of any of our achievements but for his own purpose. Before time began he planned to give us in Christ the grace to achieve this purpose, but it is only since our saviour Jesus Christ has been revealed that the method has become apparent."

God has supplied the believer with everything he needs in order to fulfill the great commission and make disciples of all nations. There is not one believer who cannot do this, or not one who has an excuse for not doing it. The reason God has equipped each individual believer with desire, spiritual gifts, talents and skills is so that we can do the work he intends for us to do. The work he intends for us to do is to make disciples using his strategy in our own unique way. In addition to our individual equipment, the text above reveals three other things God has given us in order to make our impact in the world.

Writing to Timothy, his disciple, Paul said that God has given us a purpose for which to live. From the Scriptures, we know this purpose to be the great commission to make disciples of the nations. Second, Paul said that God has given us the grace to achieve our purpose. This statement is, in effect, an open purchase order to the resources of heaven. God is standing by ready to supply whatever we need in order to get the job done. Third, Paul said that when Jesus came, he gave us a method by which we can make disciples. It is the method that believers need to learn and employ daily as we live out the purpose God has for our lives on earth.

When we looked at the great commission passage in Matthew, we found an overview statement of the process of making disciples. In Matthew, we were given three steps in this process: we are to evangelize, baptize, and train those who believe on the Lord Jesus Christ. Each one of these process parts should be studied, learned, and practiced by all believers. The third one, training, is the one we want to bring into focus in this lesson. Believers need to be trained, or prepared, for the work God has for them to do. It is the job of other believers to provide this training.

The place in the Bible where we can go to see the method of disciple-making that Jesus used is John chapter seventeen. The methodical steps in this chapter have been presented in another lesson in this series. In the present lesson, we want to consider the same method but from a different angle. Robert Coleman provided this angle in his classic work on disciple-making, The Masterplan of Evangelism. This is a little book that every believer should read and re-read, and apply in their daily life. It can be bought for the price of one fast-food meal. If you buy it, it will be perhaps the greatest monetary investment you can make into your own life and in the lives of others. The compounded interest you will receive in impact in the world through this book will be of much greater value than the six dollars you will have spent to buy it.

In The Masterplan of Evangelism, Coleman arranged Jesus's method of disciple-making into eight steps. They take us all the way from entering a mentoring relationship to actually reproducing a reproducing disciple of Christ. Let's consider each step in this process and get them anchored in our minds and hearts. I have given other labels to the steps Coleman named.

1. CHOOSE YOUR DISCIPLES

The public ministry of Jesus lasted a very short time, probably only as long as about two years and four months. When he began his ministry, he worked alone for a period of time. This gave him time to observe and evaluate the people who were following him from place to place to witness his ministry. From the crowds who followed, Jesus picked out a dozen men in whom he would invest his time and his life. He looked for potential in them which could be developed. These men would be the first wave of visionary, world-impacting, reproducing disciples made by the Lord.

2. SPEND TIME WITH THEM

This is a simple step in the process. It is the principle of presence. Jesus spent time with his followers. He built a personal relationship with each one of them. Disciple-making takes time. It is through the relationship that all the other steps can be accomplished.

3. EXPECT SOMETHING FROM THEM

Jesus expected something from those in whom he invested his life. They had to be committed to the process. If not, it could not be done. Those with whom you invest will have to be as committed as you are to the process. You are leading them to the goal of a personal world-impacting disciple-making ministry. Such a lofty goal requires and demands a deep level of commitment.

4. TEACH THEM

As Jesus spent time with his disciples, he imparted to them his purpose and plan whereby he would impact the world with the good news of the gospel. He taught them the things God had said in his Word and what he meant by what he said. He gave to them the Scriptural foundation they would need to carry out their assignments. The teaching of the Bible has to be a key component of the disciple-making strategy. This is the reason we make so much of it.

5. SHOW THEM

Jesus not only gave them the words of Scripture, he practiced them before his disciples. He showed them by living example how to live the world-impacting life. He showed them how to do the work that he was soon to deploy them to do. He revealed not only how to do it but also the cost it would require in time, preparation, development, blood, sweat, and tears, and possibly to the point of physical death.

6. ASSIGN WORK TO THEM

When the disciples had made enough progress, Jesus gave them work assignments to do. He wanted to see what they had learned and if they would follow his instructions to the letter. He was preparing them for a greater part in the ultimate role of world-conquest.

7. GUIDE THEM IN THEIR DEVELOPMENT

After the disciples had done the work Jesus delegated to them, he would check up with them and upon them to see how they did. If they needed correction, he was there to provide it. He had to make sure they were getting ready to assume their place in the overall mission.

8. MULTIPLICATION

Finally, when the disciples had developed through the entire process, Jesus was ready to turn them loose to reproduce other reproducing disciples. They could do this by following the same process Jesus had used with them. If followed to the letter, they would multiply, or reproduce reproducers.

This was the plan Jesus had to impact the world. It would be done from one person to another person. Nothing has changed for us today in this regard. This is still the method God is using to carry the story of rescue from the fall through Jesus Christ to the ends of the earth. He wants to continue this work through you. You can reproduce reproducers if you will learn and practice this same method of making disciples. Everywhere it is used it brings world-impacting results. Don't miss out on the action. You can have a part in it, too.

THE METHOD
BLOCK 6 - THEME 7 - LESSON 2 (206 OF 216)
LESSON OUTLINE

I THE MANDATE (Matthew 28:18-20)
   A. Evangelize
   B. Baptize
   C. Training

II THE METHOD
   A. John 17
   B. The Masterplan of Evangelism - by Robert Coleman
      1. Choose your disciples
      2. Spend time with them
      3. Expect something from them
      4. Teach them
      5. Show them
      6. Assign work to them
      7. Guide them in their development
      8. Multiplication

SCRIPTURES TO BROADEN YOUR UNDERSTANDING
1. Make Disciples
   Matthew 28:18-20
   John 17
   2 Timothy 2:2
   Jeremiah 1:1-10

LINES OF THEOLOGICAL CONNECTION
1. THE DOCTRINE OF DISCIPLE-MAKING
   The process of making disciples
   The practice of making disciples
   The resources for making disciples

2. CHRISTOLOGY
   Christ's two-fold work on earth: redemption and reproduction

3. ANTHROPOLOGY
   Personal world-impact through disciple-making

THE METHOD
BLOCK 6 - THEME 7 - LESSON 2 (206 OF 216)
QUESTIONS

1. What chapter in the Bible gives us Jesus' method of making disciples?

2. List the eight step summary of Christ's disciple-making method.

3. Who can use this strategy of making disciples?

4. Where can the disciple-making strategy be used?

5. Recall the things God has equipped us with in order to fulfill the great commission.

6. What are your excuses for not making disciples?

7. Will you buy Robert Coleman's The Masterplan of Evangelism and read it?

8. In whose life can you begin your ministry of disciple-making?

27. THE MODELS

THEME: DISCIPLE-MAKING

BLOCK 6 - THEME 7 - LESSON 3

LESSON AIM: Look at some of the models of disciple-making in the Bible.

SCRIPTURE: (Philippians 3:17)

"Brethren, be followers together of me, and mark them which walk so as ye have us for an ensample."

The greatest thing in life that a person can know is his reason for his existence. People often ask, "Why am I here?" They will say, "I know I am here for a purpose: I just don't know what it is." If you have ever said anything like this, you are about to have your questions answered. Our purpose for being here goes all the way back to Genesis 3:15. From this verse, we learn what God is doing in the world. After man fell into sin, God said that he would send a deliverer to rescue the fallen and to destroy the works of the devil. Jesus is that deliverer and his work on the cross accomplishes both purposes for which he came. God is right now about the business of taking the news of the rescue from the fall through Jesus to all peoples of the earth. He calls us to join him in this work. The primary means of spreading the news is person to person and this is done through the process of disciple-making. So here it is: the reason why you are here. You are here to be a disciple-maker, taking the story of Jesus as far around the globe as you can advance it. The means with which you have to do this is your life. The way you live and invest your life into this purpose will determine the degree of impact you will have had in the world. So hitch every wagon you have to this purpose. Put every egg you can get your hands on into this basket.

God is serious about disciple-making. He wants each one of us to have the same focus on this process as he has. In the Bible, God gave us the mandate to make disciples of the nations. In addition to everything else Jesus did while he was here on earth, he also gave us a method of disciple-making that every one of us can follow. He has equipped us with everything we will need to accomplish this task. If all of this were not enough, he gave us a number of examples in the Bible of people just like us who learned and lived the disciple-making process. We have the benefit to study their examples and to apply what we learn from them in our own ministries of disciple-making. We have no excuse for not being a maker of disciples.

In case there is some reluctance to do this work, it can be pointed out that most people have already engaged in a form of disciple-making without being aware of it. In other words, most of you already have some personal experience in doing this from

131

which you can apply in your spiritual influence in the lives of others. Where do we have this kind of experience? From life itself. If you have ever tried to teach anyone to do anything, you have some disciple-making experience. Think of all the ways you might have done this. Perhaps you have tried to help someone learn to tie their shoes. You showed them how to make sure the laces were in their eyes properly and evenly. You taught them to pull the laces as snug as they like to have them. You showed them how to loop and wrap and pull the laces into a bow. And there you have it: a shoe that is tied and some personal experience in disciple-making. Maybe you have helped someone with a math problem, showed someone how to cut the grass, paint a picture, paint a house, build a house, drive a car, bake a cake, make a dress, write a story, throw a baseball, catch a fish, wash a load of clothes, write a check, or wash behind their ears. In these and thousands of other ways that the everyday person goes about sharing life with other people are the experiences of disciple-making. Especially if you have raised a child, you have the experience you need to be a disciple maker. Again, you have no excuse for not doing it.

Now, with this confidence in our equipment and experience, let's briefly note some examples of disciple-making that we can study and follow. The first one is Jesus. Note three things about Jesus. One, he was discipled. The Bible shows us that Jesus submitted to the same process that he wants us to go through and use with others. Before coming to the earth as a baby, Jesus was discipled by the Father in heaven. Jesus often said that the things he did and the words he spoke were given to him by his Father. Jesus learned them from him in a process of watching, listening, learning, and doing. These are the basis disciplines of being a disciple. Second, Jesus had a process that he used with which to build disciples. We have already looked at the process in much detail. We will add here that the process should become the framework by which you size up every person you meet. You should try to determine where they are in the process when you meet them, and the steps you can take in their life to move them closer to becoming a reproducing reproducer of disciples. Finally, Jesus made disciples while he was here on earth. We know he had twelve who were his main body of disciples, but there were also many others. Jesus showed us by personal example how to invest our life into others who are able to do the same.

Another great example of disciple making is Barnabas. If we take all the things the Bible tells us about Barnabas, we have quite a profile of a disciple-maker. Let's boil down all of the Biblical information to two points about him as a model of disciple-making. First, he was an encourager. You should recall that encouragement is a spiritual gift. Barnabas built a ministry of disciple-making out of the spiritual gift of encouragement. His encouraging heart and actions opened the door of relationship into the lives of people. Once the relationship was established, Barnabas then became an equipper of disciples. He had influence among the apostles, the church in Jerusalem, and the church in Antioch as well. Two of his greatest disciples were Paul and Mark. A reading of the New Testament table of contents will show us what an impact Barnabas had as a disciple-maker through the lives and ministries of these two disciples.

Paul was discipled by Barnabas for a period of at least one year. Paul is an example of the person who is already so gifted that he just needs someone to help him get on the right track. Barnabas did this for Paul. And Paul became a visionary, world-impacting reproducer of disciples. The disciples he trained include the likes of Luke, Timothy, Titus, Silas, and Philemon. In the last chapter of Romans, a list of about forty-five individuals or groups of people are given in whom Paul had an influence. Many other names are also mentioned in his other writings. Paul wrote at

The LIFE Plan

least thirteen letters which are a part of the New Testament. His life continues to have an impact today through the letters which he wrote. Next to Jesus, Paul is the model of disciple-making in the New Testament of which we have the most information to study.

One final example is worthy of a brief note here. Luke was a great disciple-maker. We have two disciple-making letters that he wrote to a disciple named Theophilus. The first letter was evangelistic.   The second letter showed him how to get involved in the work God is doing in the world through disciple-making.

This is the purpose to which we are all called. God wants you to be a disciple-maker. This is the reason you are here. God is going to evaluate your life as a believer on if and how well you did this assignment. Don't let him down. Follow the models.

THE MODELS
BLOCK 6 - THEME 7 - LESSON 3 (207 OF 216)
LESSON OUTLINE

Models of disciple-making:

I JESUS
   A. Was discipled by the Father
   B. Gave us a process
   C. Made disciples

II BARNABAS
   A. Encourager
   B. Equipper

III PAUL
   A. Discipled by Barnabas
   B. Discipled many others

IV LUKE
   A. Discipled Theophilus
   B. Used writing as a tool for disciple-making

SCRIPTURES TO BROADEN YOUR UNDERSTANDING
1. Read the gospels, noting the discipling encounters of Jesus with others.

2. Read the New Testament letters of Paul, paying attention to how he speaks of the discipling process and how he used it in the lives of many people.

LINES OF THEOLOGICAL CONNECTION
1. THE DOCTRINE OF DISCIPLE-MAKING
   Examples of disciple-making:
   Moses and Joshua
   Elijah and Elisha
   Elisha and Gehazi
   Jesus and the twelve
   Barnabas and Paul
   Barnabas and John Mark
   Paul and Timothy
   Luke and Theophilus

THE MODELS
BLOCK 6 - THEME 7 - LESSON 3 (207 OF 216)
QUESTIONS

1. What is God's purpose for our lives at this time on the earth?

2. List some Biblical examples of disciple-making.

3. What are some ways we have experience in making disciples?

4. List some things you have tried to teach another person to do.

5. What have you learned about teaching people from your experience of trying to teach someone to do something?

6. How can you use your experience from your answer to question three above in your disciple-making ministry?

7. Are you presently discipling anyone?

8. Who is your favorite model of disciple-making from the Bible? Why?

28. YOUR MINISTRY OF DISCIPLE-MAKING

THEME: DISCIPLE-MAKING

BLOCK 6 - THEME 7 - LESSON 4

LESSON AIM: Use the unique ways God has equipped you to build your own ministry of disciple-making.

SCRIPTURE: (Philippians 4:9)

"Those things, which ye have both learned, and received, and heard, and seen in me, do: and the God of peace shall be with you."

God wants you to be a disciple-maker. He has provided everything you will need to do this. It is time to get started. Perhaps you would start a ministry of building disciples if you knew where to begin. This is what this lesson is all about. We will offer a process through which you can work and show you a place where you can take your first step toward building a ministry of making disciples. There are many places to begin and many ways to do it. This is merely one of them. If you find something that works better for you, by all means, use it. It is not necessarily the place where you begin, but that you begin, which is most important.

Let's take it from the top. God has a purpose for your life. In the LIFE lessons, we have presented God's purpose from two perspectives: his general purpose for all of us, and his specific purpose for each of us. God's general purpose for all of us is that we fulfill his great commission to make disciples of the nations. This is what he wants every believer to do with his life upon the earth. While we are all supposed to strive toward the same goal, we will all reach it in different ways. This is where the specific purpose of God for our individual life comes in. God wants us to each find the specific way that he designed us to fulfill his commission. We know what we are to do. The question becomes, "How will I do it?"

In order to determine how you will fulfill the great commission in your own unique way, a place to begin is with a personal inventory of equipment. On the mission of the Apollo 13 crew to the moon, the explosion of an oxygen tank aborted the goal to land on the moon and left the crew struggling to make it back safely to the earth. When their cabin began to fill with carbon monoxide, the engineers on earth built a special filter using only objects the crew had with them in the spacecraft. The engineers told the crew which materials to use and gave them the instructions to build a filter which would correct the problem. The filter worked and contributed to the safe return of the astronauts to the earth. In a similar way, we have the task of constructing a world-impacting ministry of disciple-making using only the equipment God has given us to work with. The first step is to take an inventory of this equipment.

The personal inventory consists of four things which we need to determine. First is the desire of our heart. Remember, the desire is a clue as to our true identity and of our specific purpose on earth. Desire helps us find out what we truly love to do and turn it into a ministry for the Lord. Again, almost anything can be made into a ministry of disciple-making.

The next step in a personal inventory is to discover your spiritual gift. Romans twelve is the place to go to begin to do this. In this chapter are listed seven predominate spiritual gifts. You have at least one of them. It is possible that you may have more than one of them, but one will be predominate. Your spiritual gift is the primary means through which the Holy Spirit empowers you to occupy the place in the body of Christ that God has selected especially for you. Your gift can be a major clue as to the kind of work and ministry God wants you to perform. You can find your gift by evaluating your service for the Lord and determining what you feel best at doing. A survey of the gifts is also helpful in making this discovery.

You may also be blessed with some kind of natural talent or talents. Your talents are one of the ways God has given you to open doors of opportunity for you to carry out your ministry. Inventory every talent that you have and make a note of them. Explore all of the possibilities these may open for you. By thinking ahead in these areas, you can anticipate opportunities for ministry and be ready for them when they arise. This will minimize your being caught by surprise or off guard, missing the opportunity to serve.

A fourth area of personal equipment is the acquired skills that you may have. In the construction business of the past, it used to be that a worker had one skill and this is all he did. He might have been a welder, or a fabricator, a crane operator, or something else. In today's market of smaller forces and diverse assignments, companies are interested in a worker who has several skills which can be employed. One worker may be a welder, a fabricator, and a crane operator all in one. The ability to multi-task is a valuable commodity in the workforce. It is also valuable in the ministry in that it also opens many doors of opportunity to serve. The more skills you have that you can do well, the broader your ministry can be, touching the lives of more people for God.

The next thing we need to get started in a ministry of disciple-making is an idea. What do we do with all of the equipment that God has given us? We need an idea to bring them all together to help us fulfill the great commission in our own way. Your idea can be anything whatsoever: almost. The only things that are off limits are things which God commands the believer to leave behind. As a simple example, we cannot make a ministry of stealing things and giving them to the needy. Many a great ministry has been born from one clever idea. Think of the shoebox ministry of Samaritan's Purse. You may have an idea that God wants you to use from which to start and build your ministry for God.

Take your idea and put it to work. You will find one of two things. Either it will work, or it will not work. If it works, you are in business. The thing you have to do next is to develop it. The idea you began with may not be the finished product. God may lead you into something bigger and better, starting from the idea you had in the beginning. Let it happen. Be aware of where your ministry is going and do not suppress it. God may want it to become exceedingly abundantly above what you thought of at first.

It is when an idea doesn't work that brings us to a critical point. Our first reactions are to scrap the idea completely, or to not try anything again because our idea failed. Both of these are bad responses. If an idea does not work, maybe we need to make some adjustments to make it work. Sometimes we have to use trial and error to find what works. If we do this and it still does not work, all is not lost. At least you gained some experience is getting a start. Chalk it up to experience and move on. When it is apparent that an idea or the adjustment of an idea is not going to work, it is alright to abandon the idea at this point. It is not, however, right to abandon the idea of trying a new idea. If an idea does not work, try another one, and another one, until you find the one that does work. This may be the process God takes you to find the idea he really wants you to use.

You can have a world-impacting ministry of disciple-making. You have the purpose and the equipment to do it. Use your idea and get started. Begin today.

YOUR MINISTRY OF DISCIPLE-MAKING
BLOCK 6 - THEME 7 - LESSON 4 (208 OF 216)
LESSON OUTLINE

I PURPOSE
   A. God's general purpose: the great commission
   B. God's specific purpose: unique to the individual

II A PERSONAL SURVEY
   A. Desire
   B. Spiritual gift
   C. Natural talents
   D. Acquired skills

III YOUR IDEA
   A. If it works - develop it
   B. If it does not work - adjust it - or try another one

SCRIPTURES TO BROADEN YOUR UNDERSTANDING
1. Barnabas used his gift of encouragement to build a ministry
   Acts 4:36-37
   Acts 9:27
   Acts 11:19-30

LINES OF THEOLOGICAL CONNECTION

1. ANTHROPOLOGY
   Building a personal ministry

2. PNEUMATOLOGY
   The empowering of the Holy Spirit for ministry

3. DISCIPLE-MAKING
   Impacting the world through building disciples

YOUR MINISTRY OF DISCIPLE-MAKING
BLOCK 6 - THEME 7 - LESSON 4 (208 OF 216)
QUESTIONS

1. What is the simple process through which you can work to find and begin a personal ministry of building disciples?

2. What four things are you seeking to find by doing a personal inventory?

3. Have you ever done a personal inventory?

4. In addition to your personal equipment, what do you need in order to begin a personal disciple-making ministry?

5. What should you do if an idea works?

6. What should you do if an idea does not work?

7. Do you have an idea for a personal ministry? What is it?

8. Have you ever shared your idea for a ministry with anyone?

29. BIBLE REFERENCES

THEME: A WORLD VIEW

BLOCK 6 - THEME 8 - LESSON 1

LESSON AIM: The Bible is filled with references to God's heart for the world.

SCRIPTURE: (John 3:14-18)

14 And as Moses lifted up the serpent in the wilderness, even so must the Son of man be lifted up: 15 That whosoever believeth in him should not perish, but have eternal life. 16 For God so loved the world, that he gave his only begotten Son, that whosoever believeth in him should not perish, but have everlasting life. 17 For God sent not his Son into the world to condemn the world; but that the world through him might be saved. 18 He that believeth on him is not condemned: but he that believeth not is condemned already, because he hath not believed in the name of the only begotten Son of God.

A football player would never be placed on a football field to play the game if he was not familiar with the field on which the game is played. He has to know where the boundaries are, where the end zones are, where the hash marks are, and how to use all of this knowledge of the field to his advantage in the game. The same principle holds true for the Christian. It is imperative that the Christian should be familiar with the field on which the game of life is played. Jesus said for the Christian, the field is the world.

Since the field is the world, we should seek to become as familiar with the world as we can. This means that we need to know something of subjects like geography, social studies, science, and language. We need to know particularly where continents and countries are located. We need to know details like the kind of government which is in place in each country, the natural resources they have, the kind of work they do, the makeup of the population, the languages they speak, their religions and the gods they worship. In addition to this we must consider how all of this information measures up to our knowledge of the gospel and of the mission of the church and the Christian in the world. This is the field on which we are to make an impact for God while we are in the world. To neglect and ignore these subjects is to miss the reason for our being here, and to lessen the possibility of the impact we can make for God in the world.

Believers in Christ must have a Biblical world view. A Biblical world view is simply to see the world as God sees it. The way God sees the world can be seen in the Scriptures which contain words like the world, peoples, nations, generations, and gentiles. When the Bible speaks of the world, there are at least four possibilities of what it can mean. World refers first to the physical world in which we live. This includes the heavens and the earth and the inhabitants of both places. Specifically, this is the created world which God has made. Next, world can refer to the governments and powers that rule the world. These are the kingdoms and empires of the world. We only have to recall the kingdoms of the world in the visions of Daniel and King Nebuchadnezzar to see this view of the world in the Bible. The third reference to the world has to do with the evil system that is in the world, the sin that draws us away from God. John identified this as the lust of the flesh, the lust of the eyes, and the pride of life. This is the world that runs counter to the life God would have us to live. It is to live for the temporal here and now rather than for the eternal future with God. This is the world from which Christ came to rescue his people. Finally, world refers to the people who live on the earth. These are the billions of inhabitants and thousands of people groups that live in every known and unknown corner of the globe. This is the world on which we are to focus our attention and our evangelistic and disciple-making efforts today.

God has a heart for the world. His heart includes all of the above ways of looking at the world. He loves the creation that he made. As he made it he said that it was good. He hates that the devil and sin have made it what it has become. He is working to rid the world of sin and to finally restore his creation so that it can never be destroyed again. He wants the kingdoms of men to live together in harmony in the wonderful world that he has made. And most of all he loves the people who live in the world and whose relationship with him was changed by the fall of man into sin. The Bible reveals God's heart for the world.

The Bible also reveals that God loved the world he made so much that he gave himself to rescue it from the fall. We could learn much about dealing with our problems on earth by looking at how God dealt with the problem of the world. After the fall, he could have focused on fixing the damage Satan had done to the physical earth. Or, he could have spent his time working out the differences between the kingdoms of the world, bringing them to get along with each other. He could have instantly removed sin from the world so that it could not continue to do its damage everywhere it goes. The important thing to see is that God dealt with all of these problems with the world by dealing with the root of all of these problems which is the fallen condition of the human heart. It is the heart of man that is the cause of these other difficulties. To solve the problem of the human heart is the way to solve these other problems. If we could learn and apply this lesson in the world today, we could rid ourselves of many of the lost causes that man tries to solve in every way except dealing with the problem of the human heart. Man's actions will only change when the heart is changed. This is what Jesus gave himself to do; to change the heart of fallen man.

A Biblical world view has a direct bearing on many things in our life, three of which we will mention now. First, it bears on how we view the people of the world. While we may look different on the outside, and while we may have different customs from those of others, and while we may speak a different language, and while there are many other ways in which we differ, at the level of the heart, people are the same the world over. We have the same needs, most importantly of which is the need to be washed clean of our sin in the eyes of God. All people, anywhere you find them, have this same need.

Our world view also bears upon our prejudices. Since peoples are different from each other, sin magnifies these differences to the point of hatred. Many times in this world, people hate other people simply because they are not like them. People groups have the tendency to favor themselves above all others. Herein lay the seeds of prejudice, persecution, war, holocaust, and annihilation. This escalating process should show us the danger of prejudice and the need to deal with it.

A Biblical world view will also bear directly upon our personal ministries for the Lord. How we view the peoples of the world will determine the extent we are willing to go to take the gospel of Jesus Christ to the lost and dying. The command of the great commission is to make disciples *of all nations*. It is to this end that we are called to do ministry. Any vision short of this is not Biblical and is in need of being corrected.

As an ongoing devotional exercise, as you read the Bible, take the time to mark verses which speak of God's heart for the world. You will see that this concept is written into every book of the Bible. There is no doubt as to how God feels about the world. The way we feel about it should measure up to this standard of measurement.

BIBLE REFERENCES
BLOCK 6 - THEME 8 - LESSON 1 (209 OF 216)
LESSON OUTLINE

I THE WORLD
  A. The physical world
  B. Governments and kingdoms
  C. The world system
  D. The peoples of the world

II GOD'S HEART FOR THE WORLD
  A. Revealed in certain words of Scripture
  B. He gave himself for the world

III A BIBLICAL WORLD VIEW
  A. People
  B. Prejudice
  C. Personal ministry

SCRIPTURES TO BROADEN YOUR UNDERSTANDING
1. Look up these Scriptures to see God's heart for the world
  Genesis 1:28
  Deuteronomy 4:9
  Psalm 2:8
  Psalm 67:1-2
  Matthew 28:18-20
  Acts 1:8
  Romans 12:1-2
  1 Thessalonians 1

2. There are too many verses to list here about God's heart for the world. Take your concordance and look up the verses which refer to peoples, generations, gentiles, and nations. This will help you gain more insight into God's heart for the world.

LINES OF THEOLOGICAL CONNECTION
1. CHRISTOLOGY
   Redemption
   The death of Christ

2. SOTERIOLOGY
   Salvation for all peoples

3. ANTHROPOLOGY
   Biblical world view
   Personal ministry
   Dealing with prejudice

4. THE DOCTRINE OF THE SCRIPTURES
   God's heart for the world in the Scriptures

BIBLE REFERENCES
BLOCK 6 - THEME 8 - LESSON 1 (209 OF 216)
QUESTIONS

1. How can we recognize God's heart for the world in the Bible?

2. Give a simple definition for a Biblical world view.

3. List four possibilities the Bible can mean when it speaks of the world.

4. What issue must be solved before we can truly solve all other issues in the world?

5. What is the remedy for the condition of the human heart?

6. How did God prove his love for the world?

7. List three things that are directly affected by our world view.

8. How is our personal ministry affected by our world view?

30. ETHNIC GROUPS

THEME: A WORLD VIEW

BLOCK 6 - THEME 8 - LESSON 2

LESSON AIM: Present the way we see people in our world view.

SCRIPTURE: (Matthew 28:18-20)

18 And Jesus came and spake unto them, saying, All power is given unto me in heaven and in earth. 19 Go ye therefore, and teach all nations, baptizing them in the name of the Father, and of the Son, and of the Holy Ghost: 20 Teaching them to observe all things whatsoever I have commanded you: and, lo, I am with you alway, even unto the end of the world. Amen.

When Jesus issued his great commission to his followers, he gave the command to make disciples of all nations. In a real sense, he has placed the weight of the world on our shoulders with this colossal task. In order to even begin to obey it, we must clarify what Jesus meant when he used the word "nations".

Our first reaction to this command is to consider the geographical or governmental nations of the world. In doing so, we think of world maps, and continents, and countries, rather than the people who live in these countries. The word Jesus used, however, is not a reference to countries but to people. The word "nations" comes from the Greek word "ethnos". We can easily see our English word "ethnic" in this word which clearly identifies people rather than geographies. The use of this word by Jesus helps us identify the target to which we are to aim, and gives us a clue as to how we must go about the huge task of reaching the peoples of the world with the gospel.

As we consider the assignment God has given to us to be his witnesses and to carry his good news to the nations of the world, we can easily be overwhelmed by the sheer numbers involved. For example, the total population of the world is close to seven and one half billion people. How can we begin to reach such a target audience when we are just one person, we have limited resources and abilities, and our life span on earth is so short? Questions like these which obviously can be quickly answered with, "It's impossible; don't even try it;" turn us away from the task before we attempt to take the first step in obeying our Lord's command. The enemy tells us, "It's too great an assignment. God expects way too much of you. There is no way you can do this. Why even try?" Too many Christians have surrendered this battle to the enemy without ever having fired one shot toward reaching the goal.

In the word "ethnos" Jesus gave us our first clue as to how we can go about the business of fulfilling his command. Seven and one half billion is a lot of people. It is an overwhelming number for sure. But if we can break it down into smaller portions, we can begin to see how we really can engage in the work and actually make progress toward completing the task God has given us to do. This is what the word "ethnos" does for us. It breaks down the population of the world into smaller portions that we call people groups.

There are conflicting statistics as to how many people groups there are in the world. Reports range from 12,000 to 16,000 different groups. When you begin to study people groups, and the things that distinguish one from the other, you can understand the difference in this number. In order to try to determine the progress the church has made in reaching the peoples of the world with the gospel, the people groups of the world are broken down into even smaller groupings. This helps us see what has been done, what is being done, and what is left to do.

People groups are typically arranged into three categories and classified as such. The first group is those people groups which have been reached with the gospel. To be considered reached means that there is an indigenous church planting movement among the group and that around two percent of the population of the group are evangelical Christians. There are some 6,800 reached people groups in the world today. This represents about three billion people of the total world's population.

A second group is called the unreached people groups of the world. Obviously, the same criterion is used to determine what an unreached people group is. In an unreached people group, there is not an indigenous church planting movement among them, and less than two present of their population are evangelical Christians. There are some 7,000 unreached people groups remaining in the world today, also claiming a total of nearly three billion people.

Another grouping of the people groups of the world is the group called unengaged people groups. These are the remaining groups of people where the church has yet to establish a foothold of evangelism and church planting efforts. There are some 2,800 unengaged people groups in the world, representing around one billion people. When we categorize the people groups of the world into these three groupings, we can see that that there is still much work to be done. We can also see where the work needs to be done. Those who are considering a call into missionary ministry should consider looking into these areas where so many people still need to hear the gospel and be taught to walk in the ways of the Lord.

As we consider the people groups among whom God is calling us to work, four things in particular distinguish one group from another. The first one obviously is race. The races can be traced all the way back to Genesis 11 when the nations were formed and scattered after the Tower of Babel incident. The races are fixed in number. Groupings among the races may fluctuate somewhat.

Location is also an important factor among a people group. Where they are located on the earth has bearing upon so much about their culture and lifestyle. Location introduces other factors like water supply, food production, climate, dress, how they go about earning a living, and threats from their neighbors and from natural disasters.

Language is one of the distinguishing marks of a people group, and perhaps the most important one. It was around language that the nations were divided at Babel in the first place. People have to be able to communicate and language obviously is how they do it. Language brings its own set of difficulties for the missionary. Some languages are spoken only, having no alphabet or writings. History is passed down orally. Other languages are spoken and written but the alphabet may be more extensive than simple letters. Certain sounds appear in some languages that are not present in others. All of these issues and more make language an important part of every people group.

Finally, the sum total of all of these mentioned and non-mentioned distinguishing characteristics is called culture. Culture can divide even the groups of people who speak the same language. All of these factors are fascinating facets of study as we begin to learn about all of the different people groups, or nations, or ethnic groups of the world.

Take a look at these resources as you begin to educate yourself on the world's ethnic groups: Operation World; www.peoplegroups.org; www.joshuaproject.net. You will be amazed as you consider the most wonderful part of God's creation: people.

ETHNIC GROUPS
BLOCK 6 - THEME 8 - LESSON 2 (210 OF 216)
LESSON OUTLINE

I OVERWHELMING NUMBERS
    A. The world's population
    B. People groups
        1. Reached people groups
        2. Unreached people groups
        3. Unengaged people groups

II PEOPLE GROUP FEATURES
    A. Race
    B. Location
    C. Language
    D. Culture

III RESOURCES
    A. Operation World
    B. www.peoplegroups.org
    C. www.joshuaproject.net

SCRIPTURES TO BROADEN YOUR UNDERSTANDING
1. Formation and scattering of the nations
Genesis 11

2. Commission to reach the nations
Matthew 28:18-20

3. Considerations about the nations
Acts 17:26-27

LINES OF THEOLOGICAL CONNECTION
1. ANTHROPOLOGY
   The nations of the world
   Cultural studies
   Linguistics studies
   The missionary call
   Personal world impact among the nations

2. THE DOCTRINE OF GOD
   God's heart for the world

3. SOTERIOLOGY
   Salvation for all peoples
   The Great Commission

4. ECCLESIOLOGY
   The purpose and mission of the church in the world today

ETHNIC GROUPS
BLOCK 6 - THEME 8 - LESSON 2 (210 OF 216)
QUESTIONS

1. What is the approximate population of the world today?

2. How many people groups make up the world's population?

3. In what three ways can we arrange the people groups of the world?

4. When is a people group considered reached with the gospel?

5. What is the combined total of unreached and unengaged people groups?

6. How many people are represented in the groups mentioned in the previous question?

7. List the four factors this lesson presented about individual people groups.

8. Would you consider serving God among an unreached or unengaged people group? Why or why not?

31. UNREACHED PEOPLE GROUPS

THEME: A WORLD VIEW

BLOCK 6 - THEME 8 - LESSON 3

LESSON AIM: Open the door to the subject of unreached people groups.

SCRIPTURE: (Psalm 96:7-9)

7 Give unto the LORD, O ye kindreds of the people, give unto the LORD glory and strength. 8 Give unto the LORD the glory due unto his name: bring an offering, and come into his courts. 9 O worship the LORD in the beauty of holiness: fear before him, all the earth.

The best one could hope to do in a two page paper on any subject is to begin to scratch the surface of an introduction. Even the simplest of subjects is a whole world of exploration, information, analysis, and application in itself, commanding volumes of information that could be written on its behalf. This has been true of all of the LIFE lessons in this plan, and is certainly reiterated in the subject at hand, the unreached peoples of the world. The best we can hope to do on so vast and so important a subject is to introduce you to it, and hopefully make it salty enough to quicken your thirst to look into the matter on your own in more detail.

Modern missionary work has taken place in three movements, beginning in the late 1700's to the present day. Moved by the Scriptural mandate of the great commission, his exposure to the peoples of the world through the journals of explorers, and by the apathy of the church of his day in this direction, William Carey, the father of modern missions, wrote a little book which propelled missionaries to take the gospel to the coasts of every continent on earth. Some one hundred and fifty years later, Hudson Taylor began a movement toward the inland areas of the continents by founding The China Inland Mission. The twentieth century has seen the movement of missions transition to a focus on the people groups which live in all of the places within the interior of the continents of the world. This is the missionary movement of which the church is a part today.

In the previous lesson, we learned the general designations of the people groups of the world by those who are planning to take the gospel to them. People groups are designated as reached, unreached, and unengaged. In this lesson, we will look at the grouping of peoples that we call unreached.

By way of definition, an unreached people group is a group of people who are connected by a common characteristic which have less than two percent of its population who are evangelical Christians. They also do not have an established church movement of their own people who can continue the work of evangelism and disciple-making among their group. They do not have enough Christ-followers and resources devoted to the work of the ministry to continue to reach their people without the help of an external witness for Christ. Some 7,000 people groups in the world totaling around three billion people are designated as unreached people groups. There is no lack of need in this area for anyone who is contemplating a call into missionary work.

No two unreached people groups are exactly alike. This is why they have an identity as a unique, distinct, and separate people group. Something about their language or culture makes them different from everyone else. Therefore, the strategy to reach them with the gospel must be tailor-made for their specific idiosyncrasies. Those who seek to evangelize and disciple an unreached people group must go to where they are, live among them, and learn their culture and language in order to be able to communicate the gospel in a way that can help them to receive it in their own setting. Naturally, this is dangerous and sacrificial work on the part of the missionary. Many of the early missionaries carried their belongings to the field in their coffins. We must understand that this is not out of the question for missionaries today.

For the believer who has a drawing toward missionary work among the unreached people groups of the world, the 10/40 window has to be a consideration. The 10/40 window, also called The Resistant Belt, is a rectangular box in the eastern hemisphere beginning at 10 degrees north latitude and extending to 40 degrees north latitude. It extends in the west to the edge of Africa, and eastward to the Far East. It includes northern Africa, the Middle East, and Asia. The 10/40 window contains 35% of the earth's global land mass; 65% of the earth's population; and 90% of the world's poorest people. Nearly five billion people live in this box which houses 95% of the unreached people groups of the world. All one has to do is to watch about one week's worth of newscasts to see what a dangerous and volatile place this is. Yet, if we are to finish the task of making disciples of the nations, someone has to be willing to go into the 10/40 window as a witness for Christ.

What if you are to be one of God's missionaries among the unreached of the world? How could you begin the process of preparation for your work among the unreached? First, begin by identifying a connection between yourself and the unreached people group. We might first think this is impossible since they are a unique group on their own. While they are distinct, there remain needs that are common to all peoples. You can begin your search by considering how the desire of your heart might be used to meet one of their needs. The meeting of this need could be the bridge that carries the gospel to them for the first time in their history.

All people groups have needs in various areas such as spiritual needs, social needs, industrial needs, and humanitarian needs. Within one of these or many other needs clusters, you may find that one thing that could connect you to an unreached people group. For example, say that you have an interest in providing clean water to those who presently have to walk miles per day and carry water back to their homes for survival. What if you could dig a well in their village or near their village which would give them better access to better water? This could be your connection that could help you take the gospel to them. The thing is to look for and find a connection between you and them, make a plan to physically connect, and follow through with your plan.

The next thing you can do right now to prepare you to minister among an unreached people group is to research the vast amount of information that is available on the subject. From your living room couch or from your hand-held mobile device, you can begin to educate yourself on the unreached peoples of the world. Whether you go or not, all Christians should do this as a means to pray for the work, the workers, and for the people who have yet to hear the good news of salvation through Jesus Christ. Take a look at the list of resources offered in the study notes of this lesson. Go to the websites and begin to learn about the unreached people groups of the world. Learn about the work that is being done to prepare people to go. Learn about those who are there right now, living among an unreached group. See what God is doing in the world today. Listen to the Holy Spirit as he speaks to you heart about the work he wants you to do to reach the unreached here, there, or anywhere they may be found. There is yet much work to do. And, workers are needed in the harvest.

UNREACHED PEOPLE GROUPS
BLOCK 6 - THEME 8 - LESSON 3 (211 OF 216)
LESSON OUTLINE

I UNREACHED PEOPLE GROUPS
   A. Definition
   B. Details

II THE 10/40 WINDOW
   A. Where it is
   B. What is in it

III PREPARING FOR MINISTRY AMONG THE UNREACHED
   A. Connecting your interests with an unreached people group
   B. Research unreached people groups

SCRIPTURES TO BROADEN YOUR UNDERSTANDING
1. Use your concordance to look up Scriptures containing the following words:
   People, nations, kindred, tribes, tongues

LINES OF THEOLOGICAL CONNECTION
1. SOTERIOLOGY
   The target of the gospel
   Salvation for all peoples through Jesus Christ

2. THE DOCTRINE OF GOD
   God's heart for the nations

3. CHURCH HISTORY
   The missionary heritage of the church
   Global evangelization

4. ANTHROPOLOGY
   Ethnic groups of the world
   Languages of the world
   Oral evangelization and disciple-making
   Unreached people groups

REFERENCES
Search the following resources on the internet.
   Operation World
   New Tribes Mission
   The US Center for World Mission
   Global Prayer Digest
   The William Carey Library
   www.peoplegroups.info
   www.frontierventures.org
   www.finishingthetask.com

LESSON GLOSSARY
1. Idiosyncrasy
   A personal peculiarity

UNREACHED PEOPLE GROUPS
BLOCK 6 - THEME 8 - LESSON 3 (211 OF 216)
QUESTIONS

1. List the three movements of modern missionary work.

2. Who is known as the father of modern missions?

3. Who is the founder of China Inland Mission?

4. Where is the 10/40 window?

5. What are the conditions within the 10/40 window?

6. What should one do to prepare for ministry among the unreached peoples of the world?

7. What interesting thing did you discover in your research about unreached people groups?

8. Do you think you would seriously consider and pray about how God might use you to do ministry among an unreached people group?

32. IMPACT THE WORLD FROM HOME

THEME: A WORLD VIEW

BLOCK 6 - THEME 8 - LESSON 4

LESSON AIM: Show how easy it is to make an impact in the world.

SCRIPTURE: (Acts 1:8)

"But ye shall receive power, after that the Holy Ghost is come upon you: and ye shall be witnesses unto me both in Jerusalem, and in all Judaea, and in Samaria, and unto the uttermost part of the earth."

There can be no mistaking the fact that God intends to send his followers into the world. The question is not, "Is God going to send me into the world?" The question is, "Where in the world does God want me to begin to make an impact for him, and to what other places does he specifically want me to have an impact?" When we are finally willing to entertain these questions, we can begin to have an impact in the world on the scale shown in Acts 1:8, and that God desires for all of his followers.

A life that makes an impact in the world can be realized when we include two catalysts for impact in our daily life. First, we must have a strategy. The Biblical strategy for impacting the world has been detailed in other places in the LIFE Plan, so we will not take the space to restate it here. Go back to those lessons and learn the Biblical strategy God has given us. It is guaranteed to give you an impact when you apply it in your life and when it is empowered by the Holy Spirit. This strategy is available to every believer.

Next, in order to make an impact in the world, we must go about it in an intentional way. We cannot simply hope and pray to have an impact without putting our hands to the plow. Sitting back and doing nothing will certainly result in time and opportunity squandered, and a life wasted before we know it. We have to take everything that we have learned and fashion it into a work that we can do intentionally everyday of our life. By being strategic and intentional, we can begin to have an impact in the world on the scale that God has given us in his Word.

When strategy and intentionality are in place in our thinking, we are ready to begin to make an impact. The all-inclusive thing that God has given us with which to impact the world is our life. This again underscores the importance of the individual in God's plans, and the role God has written for us to play in his story. In reality, this is the thing that every person on earth is seeking to find in their life. They want to know, "How can I matter in the world?" God has answered all of these questions for us in his strategic plan for world impact. The problems come when we bypass his strategy, replacing it with a substitute from the adversary.

To use our life as an instrument for world impact requires two things. First, we must open our life and our heart to others. This is the hardest thing in the world for us to do because the heart is the most vulnerable part of us. Think about it. What happened in many of those times when we opened our heart to someone? In many cases, our heart was wounded in some deep way. Who wants to go through that again and again? So, we learn to conceal our heart and hide it from everyone. But, we know that our best relationships are the ones where we can open our heart and be who we are. An open heart is one of the keys to world impact. Sure, we will receive our wounds when we live this way, but it is the quickest way to open many of the doors into the places where God wants us to make an impact.

Second, to make an impact in the world, we have to open our homes to others. Our home, and the house we live in, can become our base for global impact. See how simple God has made it for us to do this? We do not have to have a multi-million dollar facility from which to impact the world. God has already supplied us with a base to house our ministry in the home in which we live. We can look for ways to open our home in order to minister to the people God brings into our life.

If we can get this far, we can now do some things which can begin to help us make an impact in the world with the life that God has given to us. We have a strategy. We can be intentional. We can open our heart and home to others. Now, all we have to do is to get into action is some way. You might want to try some of these ideas to begin to make your impact in the world.

Begin where you are. There are many tools available to help you research the community in which you live. Use the internet to research the demographic statistics of your area. You will be surprised to find that God has already placed many opportunities very close to you in which you can increase the influence of your life. Drive around in your area and explore the locations where ministry opportunities exist. As you discover them, figure out ways that you can use them in your strategic plan for personal world impact.

Next, do something. Go to work. Look for a person to disciple. Spend some time pouring yourself into another believer. After all, this is the great commission, isn't it? Use your computer to extend your influence. Write a blog. Blog sites can be had for free on the internet. This is an opportunity to share your thoughts about God and life and Scripture. Everyone has a story to tell and a unique way in which to tell it. Take advantage of this world-impacting idea. Find a Christian pen-pal. There are great websites to help to do this as well. Correspond online with people from other countries. Learn about their life, their culture, and their beliefs. Gently interject the gospel of Jesus Christ into your correspondence and become a world-impacting evangelist without moving from your living room couch. Write and share short Bible stories that you can email to people overseas. Find ways to live out of the desire of your heart to serve the Lord by serving others in the way that God has designed you to serve. Make cross-cultural connections in your area with those who have come here from other countries. We see them everywhere we go. Step out and connect with them. Establish a friendship with them. Go home with them. Bring them to your home. There are many ways to get involved in ministry that makes an impact in the world for God. Do not miss out on this great life adventure that is right under your nose.

As you go about your work, look for ways to expand it and extend it to as many people and places as possible. Ask God to enlarge your territory, to expand your borders, to increase your impact in the world for him. Think in terms of ever-enlarging circles that will take the influence of your life as far around the world as you can send it. Think beyond your church and community to other cities, counties, states, countries and continents. Think in terms of the influence you will leave behind when your life on earth is done, and the impact your life can go on making in the world when you are gone. The sum total of Acts 1:8 is to make an impact in the world to the last person on earth, until the end of time. This is something you can do.

This is the scope of impact that God has made possible for each one of us to have. Impacting the world can be done at low cost and from our home. It can be done from where we are at any given moment. The difference maker between a life wasted and a life invested is a change in our thinking. All we have to do is to align our life with the plan of God in the world and we can make a lasting spiritual impact for him.

IMPACT THE WORLD FROM HOME
BLOCK 6 - THEME 8 - LESSON 4 (212 OF 216)
LESSON OUTLINE

I TWO CATALYSTS FOR WORLD IMPACT
   A. Strategy
   B. Intentionality

II YOUR LIFE IS YOUR MEANS OF WORLD IMPACT
   A. An open heart
   B. An open home

III WORLD-IMPACTING IDEAS
   A. Begin where you are
   B. Go to work
   C. Expand your borders

SCRIPTURES TO BROADEN YOUR UNDERSTANDING
1. Impact the world
   Psalm 2:8
   Matthew 28:18-20
   Acts 1:8
   1 Thessalonians 1

LINES OF THEOLOGICAL CONNECTION
1. THE DOCTRINE OF GOD
   God's plan to evangelize the nations

2. ANTHROPOLOGY
   Personal ministry
   Global ministry
   Demographics

IMPACT THE WORLD FROM HOME
BLOCK 6 - THEME 8 - LESSON 4 (212 OF 216)
QUESTIONS

1. What are two catalysts for impacting the world?

2. In what two ways can we begin to impact the world?

3. How can we begin to find a local place to begin a world-impacting ministry?

4. List some ways to use the internet to impact the world.

5. How can you find information on the peoples of the world in your area?

6. When you find the people of the world in your local area, what do they represent?

7. Have you recently made friends with a person from another country?

8. What are some of your ideas for impacting the world?

33. JERUSALEM - FAMILY

THEME: MAKING YOUR LIFE COUNT

BLOCK 6 - THEME 9 - LESSON 1

LESSON AIM: Begin making an impact with your life for God among the people who are closest to you.

SCRIPTURE: (Acts 1:8)

"But ye shall receive power, after that the Holy Ghost is come upon you: and ye shall be witnesses unto me both in Jerusalem, and in all Judaea, and in Samaria, and unto the uttermost part of the earth."

We have come to our final theme of The LIFE Plan Bible lessons. Our aim through these lessons has been to give you the Biblical foundation you need to help you fulfill the Lord's great commission to make disciples in all nations. We have tried to do this by emphasizing the Bible's story of why and how God sent the Messiah into the world. We have presented the Bible's structure to help you follow the story through each book of the Bible. We have taken time to present the Bible's strategy of spiritual reproduction and multiplication to give you a handle by which you can take hold of what God is doing in the world and to that which he has invited you to participate. Our final block of studies has been on how you can put all of this information together to take your place in the story God is telling. Now, our final theme is a practical guideline for setting your ministry in motion and continuing it for the rest of your life.

Acts 1:8 is one of the greatest verses in the Bible. It is a spring which gives and keeps giving rich refreshment to the thirsty student who will stay there and drink from it. Among the many wondrous things we find in this verse are the practical guidelines for how any follower of Christ can make an impact in the world for God. It gives us our part in the story God is telling by stating what God wants his followers to be and do in the world. Jesus said that we will be his witnesses. Our mission in the world can be stated in no simpler terms than this. God saved us that he might send us to be a witness of Jesus Christ. He intends for us to be a witness of Christ all over the world and in a simultaneous manner. In other words, God wants us to witness of Jesus Christ in many place around the earth all at the same time. The strategy we have presented in the LIFE lessons is the Biblical way this can be done. And, it is so simple that any believer can do it.

This verse not only tells us what to do, but also how it is to be done. We are to be global witnesses of Jesus Christ in the power of the Holy Spirit as we follow the simple strategy laid out for us in the verse. We need each one together, that is, the Spirit and the strategy, not one or the other exclusively. While this is a wonderful strategy, it cannot work by itself apart from the empowerment of the Holy Spirit. And, the Holy Spirit wants to empower us but will not do it if we have no strategic intent. Here again, God has provided that which is necessary for us to be his witnesses all over the world at the same time by providing us with a strategy to follow and with the energy of his Spirit through which we can do his will. This leaves us with no reasonable excuse for not being a world-impacting witness of the Lord Jesus Christ.

Since God has furnished us with everything we need to be his global witness, where do we begin? The practical strategy God gives us in this verse gives us both the starting place and the ultimate goal of being a witness for Christ. Jesus said that we will be his witnesses in Jerusalem, Judea, Samaria, and to the uttermost part of the earth. This four-fold strategic plan should become the practical guideline that you use from now on to take what you have learned from these lessons and to develop and expand that knowledge into your own world-sized part with Christ in his mission on earth.

This plan of God for us is simple. The first step is to begin where you are, in your own Jerusalem. Jerusalem represents two things, at least. One, it represents the location where we are at the time when we begin our world-impacting ministry for Christ. This means that we can begin to impact the world from any location on the planet. God wants us to begin where we are and expand our ministry and influence to as many places around the world as possible.

Many Christians have the idea that in order to be a global witness, we would surely have to move to another place on earth and do our ministry there. This could be God's plan for us, but not necessarily. Even if we did move to the other side of the world, God would still want our influence to make its way from there back to the side of the earth from which we departed. Therefore, we can begin from wherever we are and seek to extend our influence to other parts of the earth.

Jerusalem represents location on the earth and it also represents the people who are closest to us in our lives. In other words, we can be a global witness for Christ, beginning where we stand and among the people who are within the circles in which we move on a daily basis. For a believer, the people closest to him are usually his physical family and his church family.

Let's think first of the church family. Christ said we will be his global witnesses. Within the church, Christ has given us two ways in which we can practice being his witness. They are the church ordinances: baptism and the Lord's Supper. When we participate in these ordinances, we are witnessing of our faith in Jesus Christ. This gives us the opportunity, while we are with the family of believers, to gain some experience as a witness for Christ. We should go with this experience under our belt to witness of Christ outside the church as well. So, being a witness begins at the house of God.

We can also be a witness for Christ among our physical families on earth. In the gospels, when a person confessed his belief in Christ, Jesus often told them to go home and tell their families what had happened in their life. And, sometimes, the first thing a new believer will say is that he wants to tell someone in his family about his experience with Jesus because that person needs him in their life also. They may want to share the good news with a parent or a sibling or some other very close family member.

When we try to witness to a family member, there are two things we have to keep in mind. Our witnessing experience with a family member will more than likely be one or the other of these two things, and sometimes, both at the same time. On one hand, witnessing to family can be the most difficult place to witness for Christ, especially when you are a brand new believer. Family knows us better than anyone and it can be difficult to overcome obstacles from our past where a family member may be concerned. For any number of reasons, they may not want us to share the gospel with them. We should remember that Jesus said that a prophet has his greatest difficulty among his own people. On the other hand, a family member can be easy to witness to since we already have a good personal relationship with that person. In either case, we can gain the experience we need for witnessing to others by faithfully witnessing to our own family.

It is time for you to give it a try. Who is the family member to whom you can be a witness for Christ? Be that witness to them. You may win them to Christ.

JERUSALEM - FAMILY
BLOCK 6 - THEME 9 - LESSON 1 (213 OF 216)
LESSON OUTLINE

I OUR PART IN GOD'S STORY
    A. What we are to do
        We are to be his witnesses
        1. All over the world
        2. Simultaneously
    B. How we are to do it
        1. In the power of the Holy Spirit
        2. Strategically

II BEGIN WHERE YOU ARE
    A. Jerusalem
    B. Family
        1. Church
        2. Home

SCRIPTURES TO BROADEN YOUR UNDERSTANDING
1. Read the gospels and the Acts and pick out the personal witnessing encounters
    Matthew
    Mark
    Luke
    John
    Acts

LINES OF THEOLOGICAL CONNECTION
1. CHRISTOLOGY
   The person and work of Jesus Christ

2. SOTERIOLOGY
   The gospel of Jesus Christ

3. ECCLESIOLOGY
   Evangelism
   Witnessing to a family member

JERUSALEM - FAMILY
BLOCK 6 - THEME 9 - LESSON 1 (213 OF 216)
QUESTIONS

1. What two things mentioned in this lesson does Jesus do for us in Acts 1:8?

2. What are the two things God has provided in this verse in order for us to be a witness for Christ?

3. What word best characterizes the kind of witness we are to be for Christ?

4. How can we be a global witness for Christ?

5. Where is the best starting place for being Christ's global witness?

6. To whom should we begin to be a witness for Christ?

7. What two things should we remember when we witness to family?

8. Are you a witness for Christ among your family members?

34. JUDEA - FRIENDS

THEME: MAKING YOUR LIFE COUNT

BLOCK 6 - THEME 9 - LESSON 2

LESSON AIM: Start to move out beyond your family to impact the lives of your friends and acquaintances.

SCRIPTURE: (Acts 1:8)

"But ye shall receive power, after that the Holy Ghost is come upon you: and ye shall be witnesses unto me both in Jerusalem, and in all Judaea, and in Samaria, and unto the uttermost part of the earth."

God's plan is that every believer in Jesus Christ will be a witness for him. He wants us to be a witness on a global scale. That is, we are to make an impact in the world for Christ. Many Christians retreat when the idea of global is mentioned. Many Christians are content with having their salvation but keeping it to themselves. It would be wise for all of us to remember that our relationship with God and our mission for God go hand in hand. God does not intend to give one without the other. The very nature of our relationship with God is to invite others into it as well. Too often we take to extreme the personal aspect of our relationship with God as if it is exclusively for us. When we first see God in the Scriptures, he is in a circle of fellowship. It is into this circle of fellowship that we are invited. John said that the more that fellowship extends, the greater the joy to those who are already in it. God wants us to help enlarge the circle of fellowship be inviting others to be a part of it as well.

In Acts 1:8, God gave us a simple strategy to follow in order to be a witness for Christ. As we read it, we can easily see the expanding nature of the strategy. It has us to begin our witness for Christ where we are, but has us moving out into other places and periods of time. If you will look in your Bible maps to a map of Palestine, you will see this very well. Jerusalem is a city but Judea is the larger region where Jerusalem is found. Samaria is another region beyond Judea. God's strategy for world impact is one that is intended to take us from where we are to the ends of the earth until the end of time, as we shall see.

Judea, representing the larger area, reiterates the idea of the enlarging coasts of God's witnesses which is stated again and again throughout the Bible. Where ever we are, God wants us to settle down and build a base for world impact from that location. This does not mean that the central location will never move, but it does mean that no matter where the central location may be, it is to be the hub for an enlarging coast and for a world impacting ministry for God.

God's strategy for world impact in Acts 1:8 had us to begin to be a witness for Christ with the people closest to us. That obviously would be with our family. For most people, our families are the people who are closest and dearest to our hearts. There are some exceptions but this is the general rule. Moving out from Jerusalem into Judea in the strategy would have us to enlarge our coasts by taking our witness to the next group of people who are still close and dear to us and this would be our friends.

To be a witness among our friends can have the same characteristics of witnessing to our families. Many times, our best friends are like family to us. This means that it can be either very difficult or very easy to witness for Christ among our friends. It can be difficult because they are among those who know us best. They know our weaknesses and our failures as well as they know our victories. At times, they were compadres with us in our delinquencies. This can make it difficult to turn the corner from the past to share the good news of salvation through Jesus Christ. Difficult or not, we do not get a pass from witnessing of Jesus to our friends.

Witnessing to our friends, like family, can be easy because the relationship is already established. With our friends, we have already learned to be transparent and to share our deepest thoughts and feelings. They have been with us as we have wrestled over the issues of life. They have walked through some storms with us, making the ties very strong between us. This being the case, this makes being a witness to our friends all the more reasonable. Who would not want their friend to know the Lord and to follow him in his work in the world?

In the first two elements of the strategy for world impact, we can see the important role that is played by a personal relationship in being a witness for Christ. As we move out farther into the strategy, and farther away from our home base, the relationship becomes all the more important. We have known our family for our entire life. Most of our friends we have known as long, or at least for a long time. When we witness to people within the enlarging coasts, we do not have the luxury of the long, established relationship. Many times the relationship will have to be built before we can share the gospel with them. They want to learn to know us and to be able to trust us. This takes time. Many of our witnessing encounters will not be touch and go, but will take place over perhaps many years as we build the relationships that are strong enough bridges over which we can transport the gospel of Jesus Christ.

Another very important aspect of our witnessing ministry among our friends is that it can be a training ground for us for ministries to come. While we are in the somewhat safe environment of friendship, we can experiment with new ministries. Under amiable circumstances, we can put our ideas to work and try new things. This can give us the experience we need to know how to start a new ministry from the ground up, something we will likely have to do in the next stages of the strategy. This gives us the opportunity to take an idea, make plans, put it into action, evaluate it, and adjust it to see if it is going to work as we envisioned. This experience will help us in the next stages of the strategy when time is of the essence.

While our work and witness is done in Judea among friends, we also have the opportunity to develop and sharpen our ministries to make them more useful for God. There are two important aspects of ministries of which we need to be aware. First, most ideas for ministry are not perfect from the start. We have ideas and make plans which may or may not work. As we put them into practice, we will soon be able to see where the problems and deficiencies are, and where the adjustments need to be made.

This is the time to develop our ministries and have them ready for future deployment. A second thing to remember is that sometimes, an idea for ministry will turn out to be more than we ever dreamed of. As we develop it, God will continually guide our footsteps, leading us into the development of a ministry that we could never see coming in the beginning. Be ready to experience this with some of your very own ideas. God truly does do exceeding abundantly above all that we can ask or think.

The end result of being a believer in Christ in that we get to live in his presence for all eternity, enjoying all that he has planned for us. This is wonderful beyond the ability to comprehend at this time. However, God has also made it possible for us to live in his presence now and to join him in the work he is doing in the world. He is giving us the opportunity to make an impact in the world as a witness for Christ by following his strategy to do so. Let's use the strategy and make our impact for him.

JUDEA - FRIENDS
BLOCK 6 - THEME 9 - LESSON 2 (214 OF 216)
LESSON OUTLINE

Judea represents:

I THE LARGER AREA
    A. Enlarged coasts
    B. Be a witness and make an impact among your friends

II TRAINING GROUND
    A. Experiment
        1. With ministries
        2. With planning
    B. Sharpen

SCRIPTURES TO BROADEN YOUR UNDERSTANDING
1. Strategy for world impact
    Matthew 28:18-20
    John 17
    Acts 1:8
    I Thessalonians 1

2. Enlarging your coasts
    1 Chronicles 4:9-10
    Psalm 2:8
    Isaiah 54:2-3

LINES OF THEOLOGICAL CONNECTION
1. DISCIPLE-MAKING
   Strategy for world-impact
   The disciple-making process

2. ANTHROPOLOGY
   Personal world-impact

JUDEA - FRIENDS
BLOCK 6 - THEME 9 - LESSON 2 (214 OF 216)
QUESTIONS

1. What is the first stage in God's strategy for world impact in Acts 1:8?

2. What is the second stage in God's strategy for world impact in Acts 1:8?

3. What can make it difficult to witness to our friends?

4. What can make it easy to witness to our friends?

5. What is an important aspect of witnessing revealed in the strategy?

6. List two benefits of a witnessing ministry among our friends.

7. List two aspects of ministry of which we should be aware.

8. Are you seeking to live your life each day using God's strategy for world impact?

35. SAMARIA - FOREIGNERS

THEME: MAKING YOUR LIFE COUNT

BLOCK 6 - THEME 9 - LESSON 3

LESSON AIM: Start to move out beyond your family and friends to impact the lives of your those who are foreign to you.

SCRIPTURE: (Acts 1:8)

"But ye shall receive power, after that the Holy Ghost is come upon you: and ye shall be witnesses unto me both in Jerusalem, and in all Judaea, and in Samaria, and unto the uttermost part of the earth."

God's strategy for impacting the world in Acts 1:8 has us to begin our witness for Christ among those people with whom we have an affinity. While this can be difficult at times, it might be the easiest places we will ever have to witness for Christ. The genius of this strategy is that doing ministry among those with whom we are familiar will give us the experience and confidence we will need to take our witness into other areas which will be much more difficult and not as receptive as the people closest to us. Jesus said that we would be his witnesses in Jerusalem, Judea, and in Samaria. Jerusalem represents family. Judea represents our friends. But Samaria is a different story altogether. It represents those people who are foreign to us.

Since the fall of man in the Garden of Eden and the resulting expulsion from the Garden, man has been on the move around the earth. The nations were scattered at the Tower of Babel, setting migration into a perpetual motion. With all of this movement taking place on the planet, every people at some point in their history are likely to encounter those who are foreign to them. The United States is a nation of immigrants. It is not a rare thing anymore to encounter many different nationalities in a single day. Those who used to be foreign to us in location are now our neighbors and co-workers. Those who were once far away have now come near to our physical location. This reality has made it easier for us to have a witness for Christ among those who are foreign to us. At the same time, it has made it nearly impossible for us to ignore this part of God's strategy for world impact. Never in our history has it been easier to have an impact among those who are foreign to us than it is today. In many cases, all we have to do is to go to the house next door to ours.

Having an impact among the foreign which are near to us can be difficult, but it does not have to be. At first, it is awkward for both of us. We look different from each other. We sound different from each other. We may dress differently. We may eat different foods or prepare the same foods in much different ways. There seem to be so many things that we do not have in common with each other. These things can be barriers to hinder our relationships if we let them. What we can do, instead of letting these things become barriers, is to allow them to open the door to conversation and relationship. They can be points of interest through which we learn about each other. We can learn to appreciate our differences, allowing them to bring us together rather than keep us apart. We should not make an attempt to communicate, find it difficult, and decide to leave it alone. Like any other relationship, we will have to keep going back and keep making progress, a little each time. And over time, we can have a good relationship by which we can share a witness for Christ.

There are still those remaining on the earth which are foreign to us in far-away places. Many of these people have never heard the gospel at all or they have a need for greater discipleship in the faith. We have to go to them as well. In the book of Acts, we have the accounts of the missionary journeys of Paul and others. We have maps in the back of our Bibles tracing these journeys. We can easily read and see how God would have us to go to other places as a witness for Christ. Today, short-term mission trips have made it possible for many believers to participate in this part of the strategy to be a witness among those who are foreign to us around the earth. It is common to hear today of believers from all over the world who traverse the globe as a part of their personal plans to make an impact for God in the world. Of course, this opportunity is available to any Christian who wants to be a part of it.

Doing ministry among the foreign does not happen without encountering another huge obstacle in this area: the obstacle of prejudice. The prejudice of peoples can predate those living on the earth at a given time. In other words, people from different ethnic backgrounds may be prejudice toward each other due to things which happened many years before their birth. Prejudice, and all the other terrible things which go with it, are handed down from one generation to the next. Much prejudice, therefore, is the result of upbringing rather than personal experience. God's strategy for world impact intentionally leads us into this area in which we would not otherwise enter.

The Samaritan people were reminders to the Jews of some very dark times in the history of their nation. They were the result of the Assyrian policy of deportation and reestablishment at the time of the Assyrian captivity in 722 B.C. Foreigners who were brought into Samaria from other places mixed with the Jews who remained in the land after the Jewish deportation. Their offspring became the Samaritan people which were so despised by the Jews. Everything about them from their heritage, to their religion, to their food, was hated by the Jews. Nothing but bad blood existed between the Jews and the Samaritans from that time onward. These were the kind of obstacles which Jesus taught his followers to overcome.

There are two well-known passages of Scripture in which Jesus raised the Samaritan question. One was the parable of the Good Samaritan. To the Jews, there was no such thing as a good Samaritan. Jesus used this teaching to address a deficiency in their own Jewish way of thinking. The other passage is the encounter Jesus had with the Samaritan woman at Jacob's well. Jesus made it a point to go through Samaria. The disciples had gone away to buy food, which you recall, was despised by the Jews. Jesus, being a Jew, spoke to the woman of Samaria which was not something a Jewish man would normally do. Everything about the encounter shows how Jesus demonstrated how his followers could overcome the prejudice which had so engrained itself in their hearts. He demonstrated how we cannot allow our prejudices to be an obstacle when it comes to building relationships with the foreign, and sharing a gospel witness with them.

Things are not that much different today than they were in the time of the Bible when it comes to prejudices between ethnic groups. The same differences still exist and will always exist from one ethnic group to another. The global witness of Christ has to be wise enough to see these prejudicial obstacles and work to overcome them. God has given us a strategy to use which will guarantee us an impactful life on a global scale if we will use it. Using it means that eventually, we will have to address the problem of prejudice in our own life. We are going to spend eternity in the presence of God with the nations of the world. We should not allow prejudice to continue to rob us of a taste of heaven on earth by preventing us to have great relationships with those who are foreign to us. And, we should remember that from their perspective, we are the foreigners.

SAMARIA - FOREIGNERS
BLOCK 6 - THEME 9 - LESSON 3 (215 OF 216)
LESSON OUTLINE

Samaria represents:

I FOREIGNERS
A. Those who are near to us
B. Those who are far from us

II PREJUDICE
A. Obstacles
B. Overcoming

SCRIPTURES TO BROADEN YOUR UNDERSTANDING
1. The Samaritan prejudice
   Luke 10:30-37
   John 4:1-42

2. Paul's missionary journeys
   Acts 11-28

LINES OF THEOLOGICAL CONNECTION
1. SOTERIOLOGY
   The death of Jesus Christ
   The resurrection of Jesus Christ

2. DISCIPLE-MAKING
God's strategy for world impact

3. ANTHROPOLOGY
Prejudice between ethnic groups.
Migration
Immigration

SAMARIA - FOREIGNERS
BLOCK 6 - THEME 9 - LESSON 3 (215 OF 216)
QUESTIONS

1. List the steps in God's strategy for world impact to this point.

2. In what two ways can we encounter those who are foreign to us today?

3. What other important thing can Samaria represent in God's strategy?

4. What was the basic reason the Jews disliked the Samaritans?

5. In which two stories in the Bible did Jesus demonstrate overcoming the prejudice of the Jews toward the Samaritans?

6. Are you building relationships today with any foreigners who are near you?

7. Do you have any plans to do a short-term mission trip to a foreign people?

8. Do you have any specific prejudices toward any other people? If so, how can you overcome them?

36. UTTERMOST - FUTURE

THEME: MAKING YOUR LIFE COUNT

BLOCK 6 - THEME 9 - LESSON 4

LESSON AIM: God wants you to invest your life in such a way that it impacts those who are not yet living on the earth.

SCRIPTURE: (Acts 1:8)

"But ye shall receive power, after that the Holy Ghost is come upon you: and ye shall be witnesses unto me both in Jerusalem, and in all Judaea, and in Samaria, and unto the uttermost part of the earth."

God fully intends to send his followers into the world as a witness of the Lord Jesus Christ. It is imperative that we who are his followers admit this intention, accept it, and make every adjustment necessary that we might fulfill it with our lives. Anything short of this is to miss God's intention for his people, and to miss the opportunity to work with God as he goes about his work in the world of reaching the lost with the gospel.

God has done everything necessary to see that we are successful in the work he has invited us to do. Acts 1:8 reveals God's strategy of world impact as a global witness for Christ. It gives us a step-by-step process to follow which will take us from where we are to the point of not only a global impact but of a generational impact as well. Let's recall the steps of the strategy that we have already learned and add the final step in the process.

Jesus said that his followers would be his witnesses both in Jerusalem, and in Judea, and in Samaria, and unto the uttermost part of the earth. This is a simultaneous process rather than a consecutive one. It requires multi-tasking on the part of the global witness. We are to be a witness for Christ in all of these places at the same time. The only way to do this is to follow the strategy and to reproduce spiritually. The starting place is in our Jerusalem. We said that Jerusalem represents our family; the people to whom we are the closest on earth. It is in the place where we are known the most that we are to begin our own world-impacting ministry for Christ. Another thing this does for us is that it gets us used to the habit of being real. We cannot hide behind a mask from those who know us the best. The tendency to do this will be greater among those who know us the least. Therefore, God takes away this option from us at the very beginning of our global witness by making us face reality. Doing this from the start will help us not to do it later.

Next we are to be a witness for Christ among our friends. This is the next natural wave of influence we have in the world. Like family, our friends know us best, giving us more experience in witnessing for Christ without the strong opposition which we will encounter in the third wave of global witnessing. The third wave is that we are to be Christ's witnesses among the foreign. We can do this from where we live and by going to places and to peoples beyond our borders. All three of these steps in God's strategy for world impact will reap a harvest to some degree which we will be able to see during our lifetime on earth.

The final step in the process will take us into another dimension of life that few Christians ever consider. God gives us the possibility that our life can go on making an impact for Christ after we leave the world. Jesus said you will be by witnesses to the uttermost part of the earth. The word *uttermost* is the Greek word *eschatos*. It means "to the last", or "to the end". This is the word from which we get our doctrine of eschatology in theology. Eschatology is the study of last things. Therefore, being a witness for Christ to the uttermost part of the earth gives us two realms in which we can make an impact for Christ. We can impact the world for Christ to the farthest places on earth, and into the future, to the end of the age. In order to have an impact into the future generations of people on earth, we have to build people now, while we are living, who can represent us after we are gone. This is exactly what Jesus did while he was here on earth, what he taught his disciples to do, and what he expects us to do as well. This is what the Bible means by calling it everlasting life. God has made it possible for our lives to go on making an impact in the world after we are gone. Take the Apostle Paul for example. Although he has been in heaven for some two thousand years, his life is still impacting the world for Christ through the continuing results of his disciple-making ministry, and through the writings he left behind. This level of life does not happen by itself. It has to be done intentionally and strategically. To the level of intent and strategy that we live our lives, will the impact of our lives be realized into future generations. God's strategy for world impact covers all the bases. It is the wise witness of Christ who learns it and lives it as long as he has breath upon this earth.

In the next few minutes that it takes you to complete the reading of this lesson, you will have finished The LIFE Plan Bible Study Lessons. Over the course of two hundred and sixteen lessons, we have tried to equip you with four things which will help you to make your impact in the world as a disciple of and witness for the Lord Jesus Christ. We have tried to give you the story of the Bible. The story of the Bible unfolds around the plot given to us in Genesis 3:15. After the fall, God told us that he would send a deliverer to rescue the fallen and to destroy the works of the devil. That deliverer was Jesus Christ and the Bible is the story of how God brought him to the earth through the Jewish nation. We have tried to share with you the structure of the Bible which supports the story that God is telling. By understanding the groups into which the Scriptures have been gathered, we can better understand how the story has been presented to us in the Word of God. We have also tried to help you see the strategy of God's Word which is presented throughout the entire Bible: the strategy of spiritual reproduction and disciple-making. From God's first command to multiply and replenish the earth, to the Lord's great commission to make disciples in all nations, God has given us the mandate, models, and method of spiritual reproduction in the Bible. Because of such prolific presentation of this strategy in the Word of God, we are completely without excuse for not using it to make our impact in the world for Christ.

This brings us to the fourth and final thing we have tried to give you in the LIFE Lessons. We have tried to help you see that God wants you to have a world-sized part with him through your personal service to the Lord. God has given you a place in the body of Christ. He has given you a role to fill and a part to play. He has work planned for you that only you can do. We have tried to point you to some starting places and to help you see the clues that God has given you that you might discover his specific purpose for your life. We are confident from the Word of God and from our personal experience in the journey of life, that the instructions we have given to you will help you find your way. At this point, the choice is yours what you will do with this instruction. You can read it and mark it off your list of studies completed. Or, you can apply it to your life and live the life God has always had in mind for you to live. Our prayer is that you will live an abundant and everlasting life in Christ as his global witness to the ends of the earth until the end of time. Happy Living.

UTTERMOST - FUTURE
BLOCK 6 - THEME 9 - LESSON 4 (216 OF 216)
LESSON OUTLINE

I GOD'S STRATEGY OF WORLD IMPACT
   A. Jerusalem - Family
   B. Judea - Friends
   C. Samaria - Foreign
   D. Uttermost - Future

II THE LIFE PLAN OVERVIEW
   A. The story of the Bible
   B. The structure of the Bible
   C. The strategy of the Bible
   D. Your service to God

UTTERMOST - FUTURE
BLOCK 6 - THEME 9 - LESSON 4 (216 OF 216)
QUESTIONS

1. How has The LIFE Plan helped you in your walk with God?

2. Would you say that you are on your way to discovering God's specific purpose for your life?

3. Would you be willing to lead others through The LIFE Plan?

4. What will you do now as a result of having studied The LIFE Plan?

5. What things did you learn from The LIFE Plan that you did not know?

6. Which LIFE lessons were your favorites?

7. Would you recommend The LIFE Plan to another person?

ANSWERS KEY TO LESSON QUESTIONS

CHAPTER 1
QUESTIONS ANSWER KEY

1. What are some beautiful sights you have seen in the created world?
Students answer.

2. Name some things that you enjoy about people.
Students answer.

3. Do you know your own ethnic background?
Students answer.

4. List some of the ethnic groups in your community.
Students answer.

5. Sin is devastating, not simply because of the things we do, but because of the condition into which we are born. List three results of our sinful condition.
In sin, we are spiritually dead, separated from God, and unable to come to God on our own.

6. What is the only solution God will accept for our sin problem?
Jesus Christ and his death is the only sacrifice for man's sin that God accepts.

7. How does God's solution for our sin problem come to us?
We are saved by grace, through faith in Christ.

8. Jesus died on the cross for our sins and he arose from the dead. The Bible calls this the gospel, or good news. List two ways that God moves us to respond to the gospel.
We have to believe on Jesus in our heart, and we have to confess Jesus with our mouth.

9. Have you believed on Jesus for salvation?
Students answer.

10. Would you like to speak with someone about your decision to trust Christ?
Students answer.

CHAPTER 2
QUESTIONS ANSWER KEY

1. After we believe in Jesus Christ in our heart and receive his salvation, we must begin to grow spiritually. List some different ways we refer to this process of spiritual growth.
   a. Growing in Christ
   b. Spiritual growth
   c. Spiritual development
   d. Maturing in Christ
   e. Discipleship

2. What is a disciple of Christ? A disciple of Christ is:
   a. A learner
   b. A follower

3. What one thing is our key to spiritual growth?
   The Bible

4. How did the Bible come to us?
   a. From God
   b. Through Man

5. How does the Holy Spirit help us to understand the Bible?
   By illumination - giving us spiritual light in order to see and understand.

6. What kind of attitude should we have when we come to read and study the Bible?
   With humility and dependence upon God

7. What two words describe the Bible as food for our spiritual growth?
   a. Milk
   b. Meat

8. What kind of spiritual food from question 7 above do you need at this time in your life? Student response

9. List 4 things the Bible is for us to help us grow spiritually.
   a. Doctrine
   b. Reproof
   c. Correction
   d. Instruction

10. List 5 things we need to do with our Bible to grow spiritually.
    a. Read it
    b. Believe it
    c. Study it
    d. Discuss it
    e. Apply it

11. Do you have a copy of the Bible? If not, please let us know.
    Student response

CHAPTER 3
QUESTIONS ANSWER KEY

1. What is the best way to begin to understand God's purpose for your life?
   In relation to the church

2. List the two bodies of Christ in the world.
   a. His physical body.
   b. His spiritual body - the church.

3. What is God's purpose for the church?
   To take the gospel to the nations.

4. What are the two areas in which we can think of the purpose of God?
   a. His general purpose.
   b. His specific purpose.

5. What is another phrase for God's general purpose?
   The Great Commission

6. List two ways to take the gospel to the nations.
   a. The nations come to us
   b. We can go to the nations

7. What are we referring to by the phrase, the specific purpose of God?
   The way an individual will fulfill the great commission

8. List four clues that will help you discover God's specific purpose for your life.
   a. Desire
   b. Spiritual gift
   c. Relationship with a disciple-maker
   d. Personal Bible study

9. Have you discovered God's specific purpose for your life? If so, what is it?
   Student response

10. What kind of ministry would you like to be involved in?
    Student response

CHAPTER 4
QUESTIONS ANSWER KEY

1. We all at times have done things to decrease God's value in the world. Are you seeking now to increase God's value in the world, and if so, how?
   Student response

2. Can you name a person who has had a spiritual influence in your life?
   Student response

3. Who do you know that would be willing to have you make a spiritual investment into their life?
   Student response

4. What will you do to make an effort to make that investment into their life?
Student response

CHAPTER 5
QUESTIONS ANSWER KEY

1. Where do we feel the effects of sin?
Inwardly and outwardly

2. What are some examples of the inward effects of sin?
Low self-worth; feel of little or no value; no purpose or direction in life

3. What inward or outward effects of sin might you be dealing with today?
Student response

4. As you read Job 1-2, what is your reaction to the destructive power of the devil in a person's life?
Student response

5. List the four facts mentioned in this lesson about being a child of God.
New birth; grow in Christ; relationship with the devil broken; access to God

6. Are you growing in Christ as a child of God? Give some evidence of your growth.
Student response

CHAPTER 6
QUESTIONS ANSWER KEY

1. What does it mean to us to know God and to become a Christian?
It means that God has given us a new beginning in life

2. Have you believed on Jesus in your heart in order to have this new beginning?
Student response

3. The Scripture tells us that we do not have to be a slave to sin. What does this news do for you?
Student response

4. God wants us to have friends who do not know him so we can share the gospel with them. Among your lost friends, who has more influence in the other one's life; you or them?
Student response

5. What are some ways you experience the struggle between the old man and the new man?
Student response

6. What should you do when you sin?
   Confess and repent

7. How are you working with God in his work right now?
   Student response

8. Do you have any plans for your future work with God?
   Student response

CHAPTER 7
QUESTIONS ANSWER KEY

1. What does it mean to be under God's condemnation?
   We are lost, have no relationship with God, and will bear the penalty of our sin unless we believe on the Lord Jesus Christ

2. What is the punishment related to God's condemnation?
   Eternal separation from God and torment in the lake of fire

3. How does one escape God's condemnation?
   By believing on the Lord Jesus Christ

4. Why does the devil want to use guilt against you?
   To keep you from reaching your potential for Christ

5. What is our standing before God based upon?
   The righteousness of Christ

6. To be pronounced not guilty by God makes us free to work for him. What work are you doing for God with your life?
   Student response

CHAPTER 8
QUESTIONS ANSWER KEY

1. According to the Bible, God's salvation is eternal. What weapon does the devil use against us when it comes to being sure of our salvation?
   He causes us to doubt our salvation

2. Why should we not doubt our salvation?
   The Bible teaches us that it is eternal; If we doubt, we cannot fulfill our assignment from God

3. Has the enemy ever caused you to doubt your salvation in Christ? What do you do when you are tempted to doubt?
   Student response

4. What do you think about God choosing you even before he made the world?
Student response

5. Why is the role of the Holy Spirit important in our salvation?
We could not confess Jesus as Lord without his help

6. Have you believed on Jesus for salvation?
Student response

CHAPTER 9
QUESTIONS ANSWER KEY
1. Where is our foundation for holiness found?
In God

2. In a word, what is the process called for making us holy?
Sanctification

3. What clue has God placed within us to help us find our purpose in life and where do we find it?
Desire - in our heart

4. What question can we ask ourself to begin to discover the desire of our hearts?
What do you want?

5. How would you answer the question, "what do you want?"
Student response

6. There is one great practical reason why we need to sanctify ourselves to the Lord. What is it?
For the benefit of others who are following us

7. Have you made a commitment to live your life for God? If not, now is a great time to do so.
Student response

CHAPTER 10
QUESTIONS ANSWER KEY
1. Why is it possible for us to see from God's point of view?
Because the Holy Spirit lives within us

2. There are many wonderful things in the world to pursue. Why should we be careful about these pursuits?
They may not be what God wants us to pursue with our life

3. By what term do we refer to God's general purpose for all Christians?
The great commission

4. What is the great commission?
Making disciples of all nations

5. Why is it important to discover the desire of your heart?
Our desire matches God's specific purpose for our life

6. What do you know about the desire of your heart?
Student response

7. What do you enjoy doing from which you could develop a ministry of disciple-making?
Student response

CHAPTER 11
QUESTIONS ANSWER KEY

1. What is our greatest need after salvation?
To see from God's point of view

2. List the three things Paul prayed that we would see from God's point of view.
God's purpose for our life; our potential; God's power

3. Potential is related to our _____ to God.
Value

4. In this passage, when Paul uses the word, "inheritance", to what is he referring?
Our value to God

5. From God's point of view, you are equal in value to _____ _____.
What does this mean to you?
Jesus Christ; Student response

6. What things have happened in your life to rob you of the knowledge and belief that you have value as a person?
Student response

7. From the things you listed in question six, what are you willing to let go of in order to see and pursue your potential for God in the world?
Student response

8. What steps will you take today to pursue your potential?
Student response

CHAPTER 12
QUESTIONS ANSWER KEY

1. List two areas where James and John intended to use God's power in the wrong way.
   Manner of use; motive for use

2. Why does God not use his power in the same way in all our lives?
   His power is unique to the servant of God and to his situation

3. Have you had an experience of calling on God to empower you to do his will? What happened?
   Student response

4. What is a great mistake we make concerning the power of God?
   Many times, we do not call upon it at all

CHAPTER 13
QUESTIONS ANSWER KEY

1. Write out God's general purpose for every Christian and its Bible reference.
   We are to make disciples of all nations (Matthew 28:18-20)

2. What is the label we have given this purpose of God for our lives?
   The great commission

3. Is any Christian exempt from fulfilling the great commission?
   No

4. What is the simple answer as to why Christians do not obey the great commission?
   They have never seen anyone model it; they have not been discipled, or taught, to reproduce other disciples of Christ

5. Where does disciple-making begin?
   With evangelism; sharing the gospel and leading a person to Christ

6. As a student in the LIFE Plan, you are being discipled with the necessary tools that will enable you to fulfill God's general purpose for your life. Will you make a personal commitment to God that you will learn this information and obey his commission?
   Student response

7. God fully expects you to be a maker of disciples. Think about your present relationships. Who do you know right now that you can begin to disciple?
   Student response

8. You come into contact everyday with people you do not know. Of these, who is God leading you to begin a personal relationship with that can be used for making disciples?
   Student response

CHAPTER 14
QUESTIONS ANSWER KEY

1. What was Jesus' purpose in appearing and disappearing before the disciples in the days following his resurrection?
He wanted them to be aware of his presence with them when they could not see him as much as they were aware of it when they could see him

2. What is another term for regeneration?
The new birth

3. What is regeneration, or, the new birth?
It is a resurrection of our dead spirit done by the Holy Spirit when he indwells the believer

4. What does the name Emmanuel mean?
God with us

5. What is the main reason God's presence cannot be experienced in some churches?
They are not fulfilling God's commission to make disciples in all nations

6. Do you experience a lack of the presence of God in your life? Why do you think this is?
Student response

CHAPTER 15
QUESTIONS ANSWER KEY

1. What is the number one reason why we should share the gospel with the lost?
Jesus commanded us to do so

2. List some obstacles to sharing the gospel.
People groups; languages; no Bible in languages; accessibility; approachability; obedience; small work force; resources

3. When you think about the billions who are without God in the world, what can you do to help the situation?
Witness to and win the ones you can win

4. Have you ever personally won a soul to Christ by sharing the gospel with them?
Student response

5. Do you know anyone personally who needs to know Christ? Who are they, and are you willing to share the gospel with them?
Student response

6. How does evangelism and disciple-making work together?
We have to win them to disciple them

7. What is the greatest reason so many people are still without God in the world?
   The disobedience of Christians to evangelism

8. Will you be willing to set a goal to win at least one person to God?
   Student response

CHAPTER 16
QUESTIONS ANSWER KEY
1. How many different cultures are there in the world?
   As many as there are people groups

2. From an evangelistic perspective, what is so important about a people's culture?
   It reveals how and what they think about the world and ways in which we may communicate the gospel to them

3. What are some cultural peculiarities about your culture?
   Student response

4. How would your answer from the previous question help or hinder someone sharing the gospel with you?
   Student response

5. Have you had any interaction with anyone from another ethnic group?
   Student response

6. What are some of the cultural differences you have noted between them and you?
   Student response

7. Have you tried to share the gospel of Jesus Christ with them?
   Student response

8. Have you discovered anything about their culture that could be an inroad for the gospel into their life?
   Student response

CHAPTER 17
QUESTIONS ANSWER KEY
1. According to Genesis 3:15, what is the work of Jesus in the world?
   To rescue fallen men; to destroy the works of the devil

2. In what two ways can we consider God's purpose for our lives on earth?
   His general purpose; His specific purpose

3. What is the difference between God's general purpose and his specific purpose?
   God's general purpose: the same for all of us - to make disciples of all nations
   God's specific purpose: the way we as individuals will accomplish God's general purpose - will vary from person to person

4. List the two reasons why God saved us.
   To be with him; to send us to preach (share the good news of redemption through Christ)

5. What does it mean, "to be with God"?
   To have a personal, and intimate relationship with him

6. What two additional things do we need to remember from this lesson?
   Our private life with God prepares us for our life in public for God.
   Our public life for God will never rise above our private life with God.

7. Do you spend time with God on an individual basis?
   Student response

8. Do you have an idea of God's specific purpose for your life?
   Student response

CHAPTER 18
QUESTIONS ANSWER KEY

1. What is God's general purpose for every believer?
   To make disciples of all nations

2. What is the purpose of the specific purpose God has for each believer?
   The specific purpose is the particular way each individual believer will fulfill the great commission

3. What clues has God given us to help us discover his specific purpose for our life?
   The desire of our heart; our spiritual gift(s)

4. What is the desire of your heart? (what you would really like to do with your life for God)
   Student response

5. What is your spiritual gift?
   Student response

6. How can you use your gift to create a disciple-making ministry for God?
   Student response

7. Have you discovered your specific purpose?
   Student response

8. Are you living each day according to God's specific purpose for your life?
   Student response

CHAPTER 19
QUESTIONS ANSWER KEY
1. List the three steps to a personal ministry.
   Discover your spiritual gift; discover your heart's desire; start a ministry based on the previous two

2. What cannot be used as a personal ministry?
   Anything the Bible condemns

3. Have you discovered your spiritual gift?
   Student response

4. Why is the heart important?
   It is central to everything else

5. What clue has God placed within our heart?
   Desire

6. Is there anything you would like to develop into a ministry for Christ?
   Student response

7. How could you use your idea for a ministry to fulfill the great commission to make disciples?
   Student response

8. What do you need to get your ministry idea off the ground?
   Student response

CHAPTER 20
QUESTIONS ANSWER KEY
1. What are the three steps to help you start a ministry for the Lord.
   Get an idea for ministry; do your research: launch it

2. What kind of help can we get for our ministry from the Bible?
   Goal, guidance, theme verse, case studies, directions

3. What things should be included in our research for a personal ministry?
   Biblical support, target, plans, helpers

4. Who are among the helpers we need for our ministry?
   Counselors, contributors, crew members

5. List the four-part cycle that helps us get our ministry running properly.
Try it, evaluate it, adjust it, try it again

6. Do you have an idea for a personal ministry? What is it?
Student response

7. With whom can you talk that can help you develop your ministry idea?
Student response

8. Are you willing to step out and give your ministry idea a try?
Student response

CHAPTER 21
QUESTIONS ANSWER KEY
1. Why should we read the Word of God?
To learn to fear the Lord and obey his word

2. List four benefits from reading the Word of God.
Combats pride; keeps us on God's path; prolongs our life and work; continues through our offspring

3. Is Bible reading a part of your regular routine?
Student response

4. Have you ever read the Bible all the way through?
Student response

5. Why should you read the Bible again and again?
Student response

6. Share some way or ways that your Bible reading has helped you in your life.
Student response

7. What difficulty do you find in reading the Bible?
Student response

8. Who can you encourage to begin reading the Bible?
Student response

CHAPTER 22
QUESTIONS ANSWER KEY
1. Do you presently own any of the books listed in this lesson?
Student response

2. Have you discovered where you can have access to these reference tools such as online or in your church library?
Student response

3. Do you make regular use of these tools in your study of the Bible?
Student response

4. What are your favorite Bible Study tools?
Student response

CHAPTER 23
QUESTIONS ANSWER KEY
1. List four benefits of memorizing Scripture.
Helps us to meditate in the Word; guards our heart, helps in spiritual warfare; helps us witness for Christ

2. What benefit do we get from meditating on the Word of God?
It helps us connect the Scriptures with each other; helps us understand the truth; helps us in self-examination

3. How can the Holy Spirit help us either in spiritual warfare or in a witnessing opportunity?
He can call up a Scripture from our memory that will meet the need of the moment

4. Share a time when the Holy Spirit gave you a verse to use in a time of need.
Student response

5. Is Scripture memory a part of your spiritual disciplines?
Student response

6. What important verses do you need to hide in your heart beginning today?
Student response

CHAPTER 24
QUESTIONS ANSWER KEY
1. What are the three simple perspectives from which Jesus taught us to pray?
Look up, look around, look ahead

2. What is the first thing we should do in prayer?
Acknowledge God

3. What things did Jesus teach us to include in our prayers when we look around?
God's plans; God's provisions; relationships; spiritual warfare.

4. What are the two battlefields on which a believer must wage spiritual warfare?
The war within; the war without

5. Where is the battle fought on the inside?
In the mind, with our thoughts

6. How do we commune with God?
Through the Word of God and prayer

7. Is prayer a part of your daily discipline?
Student response

CHAPTER 25
QUESTIONS ANSWER KEY

1. What is the basic command of the great commission?
To make disciples of the nations

2. What is the difference between evangelism and disciple-making?
Evangelism is sharing the gospel in hopes that a person will believe and be saved;
Disciple-making is training a person after they are saved

3. Where can disciple-making be done?
Anywhere

4. Why is evangelism not an end in itself?
Evangelism is one step in a larger process

5. Who is to do the work of evangelism?
Every believer

6. Who is to do the work of disciple-making?
Every believer

7. Is God's purpose any different today from that of the believers in the first century?
No

8. List the three steps in the disciple-making process from Matthew 28.
Evangelize, baptize, train

CHAPTER 26
QUESTIONS ANSWER KEY

1. What chapter in the Bible gives us Jesus' method of making disciples?
John 17

2. List the eight step summary of Christ's disciple-making method.
   Choose your disciples, Spend time with them, Expect something from them, Teach them, Show them, Assign work to them, Guide them in their development, Multiplication

3. Who can use this strategy of making disciples?
   Anyone

4. Where can the disciple-making strategy be used?
   Anywhere

5. Recall the things God has equipped us with in order to fulfill the great commission.
   Desire, spiritual gift, talents, skills, purpose, grace to achieve the purpose, a method for building disciples

6. What are your excuses for not making disciples?
   Student response

7. Will you buy Robert Coleman's The Masterplan of Evangelism and read it?
   Student response

8. In whose life can you begin your ministry of disciple-making?
   Student response

CHAPTER 27
QUESTIONS ANSWER KEY
1. What is God's purpose for our lives at this time on the earth?
   To make disciples of the nations

2. List some Biblical examples of disciple-making.
   Moses and Joshua, Elijah and Elisha, Elisha and Gehazi, Jesus and the twelve, Barnabas and Paul, Barnabas and John Mark, Paul and Timothy, Luke and Theophilus

3. What are some ways we have experience in making disciples?
   By teaching another person to do anything

4. List some things you have tried to teach another person to do.
   Student response

5. What have you learned about teaching people from your experience of trying to teach someone to do something?
   Student response

6. How can you use your experience from your answer to question three above in your disciple-making ministry?
   Student response

7. Are you presently discipling anyone?
   Student response

8. Who is your favorite model of disciple-making from the Bible? Why?
   Student response

CHAPTER 28
QUESTIONS ANSWER KEY

1. What is the simple process through which you can work to find and begin a personal ministry of building disciples?
   Know God's general purpose; find God's specific purpose; do a personal inventory; begin with an idea

2. What four things are you seeking to find by doing a personal inventory?
   Your heart's desire; spiritual gift; talents; skills

3. Have you ever done a personal inventory?
   Student response

4. In addition to your personal equipment, what do you need in order to begin a personal disciple-making ministry?
   An idea

5. What should you do if an idea works?
   Develop it

6. What should you do if an idea does not work?
   Adjust it; try another idea

7. Do you have an idea for a personal ministry? What is it?
   Student response

8. Have you ever shared your idea for a ministry with anyone?
   Student response

CHAPTER 29
QUESTIONS ANSWER KEY

1. How can we recognize God's heart for the world in the Bible?
   In words like world, peoples, nations, generations, gentiles, etc...

2. Give a simple definition for a Biblical world view.
   Seeing the world as God sees it

3. List four possibilities the Bible can mean when it speaks of the world.
   The physical world, kingdoms, the sinful world system, and peoples

4. What issue must be solved before we can truly solve all other issues in the world?
   The condition of the human heart

5. What is the remedy for the condition of the human heart?
   Salvation through Jesus Christ

6. How did God prove his love for the world?
   By giving himself for it

7. List three things that are directly affected by our world view.
   How we view the people of the world; our prejudices; our personal ministry

8. How is our personal ministry affected by our world view?
   It determines the extent we are willing to go to rescue the fallen

CHAPTER 30
QUESTIONS ANSWER KEY
1. What is the approximate population of the world today?
   7.5 billion people

2. How many people groups make up the world's population?
   12,000 to 16,000

3. In what three ways can we arrange the people groups of the world?
   Reached; Unreached; Unengaged

4. When is a people group considered reached with the gospel?
   When it has an indigenous church planting movement and when 2% of the group
   are evangelical Christians

5. What is the combined total of unreached and unengaged people groups?
   9,800 groups

6. How many people are represented in the groups mentioned in the previous
   question?
   About 4 billion people

7. List the four factors this lesson presented about individual people groups.
   Race, Location, Language, Culture

8. Would you consider serving God among an unreached or unengaged people group?
   Why or why not?
   Student response

CHAPTER 31
QUESTIONS ANSWER KEY

1. List the three movements of modern missionary work.
   Coastal; Inland; People groups

2. Who is known as the father of modern missions?
   William Carey

3. Who is the founder of China Inland Mission?
   Hudson Taylor

4. Where is the 10/40 window?
   The 10/40 window, also called The Resistant Belt, is a rectangular box in the eastern hemisphere beginning at 10 degrees north latitude and extending to 40 degrees north latitude. It extends in the west to the edge of Africa, and to the Far East to China's coast. It includes northern Africa, the Middle East, and Asia.

5. What are the conditions within the 10/40 window?
   The 10/40 window contains 35% of the earth's global land mass; 65% of the earth's population; and 90% of the world's poorest people. Nearly five billion people live in this box which houses 95% of the unreached people groups of the world.

6. What should one do to prepare for ministry among the unreached peoples of the world?
   Connect a personal interest to an unreached people group; research UPG's

7. What interesting thing did you discover in your research about unreached people groups?
   Student response

8. Do you think you would seriously consider and pray about how God might use you to do ministry among an unreached people group?
   Student response

CHAPTER 32
QUESTIONS ANSWER KEY

1. What are two catalysts for impacting the world?
   Strategy; Intentionality

2. In what two ways can we begin to impact the world?
   Open our heart; open our home

3. How can we begin to find a local place to begin a world-impacting ministry?
   Research; Exploration

4. List some ways to use the internet to impact the world.
   Research; Blog; Pen pal

5. How can you find information on the peoples of the world in your area?
Research local demographics

6. When you find the people of the world in your local area, what do they represent?
Cross-cultural opportunities for a world-impacting ministry

7. Have you recently made friends with a person from another country?
Student response;

8. What are some of your ideas for impacting the world?
Student response

CHAPTER 33
QUESTIONS ANSWER KEY

1. What two things mentioned in this lesson does Jesus do for us in Acts 1:8?
He tells us what to do - to be his witnesses
He tells us how to do it - by extending our influence around the world

2. What are the two things God has provided in this verse in order for us to be a witness for Christ?
The empowerment of the Holy Spirit; a strategy to use

3. What word best characterizes the kind of witness we are to be for Christ?
Global

4. How can we be a global witness for Christ?
By being his witness in many places simultaneously

5. Where is the best starting place for being Christ's global witness?
Where ever we are when we begin our ministry

6. To whom should we begin to be a witness for Christ?
With our family

7. What two things should we remember when we witness to family?
It might be very difficult; It could be easier since we already have a relationship with them

8. Are you a witness for Christ among your family members?
Student response

CHAPTER 34
QUESTIONS ANSWER KEY

1. What is the first stage in God's strategy for world impact in Acts 1:8?
Jerusalem - Family

2. What is the second stage in God's strategy for world impact in Acts 1:8?
   Judea - Friends

3. What can make it difficult to witness to our friends?
   They know us very well

4. What can make it easy to witness to our friends?
   We already have a relationship established with them.

5. What is an important aspect of witnessing revealed in the strategy?
   The personal relationship

6. List two benefits of a witnessing ministry among our friends.
   It gives us the opportunity to experiment with our ministries; It gives us the opportunity to develop or sharpen our ministries

7. List two aspects of ministry of which we should be aware.
   No ministry is perfect from the start; Some of our ideas for ministry will become more than we thought they could be

8. Are you seeking to live your life each day using God's strategy for world impact?
   Student response

CHAPTER 35
QUESTIONS ANSWER KEY

1. List the steps in God's strategy for world impact to this point.
   Jerusalem - Family; Judea - Friends; Samaria - Foreigners

2. In what two ways can we encounter those who are foreign to us today?
   Those who live near to us; Go to other places as a witness for Christ

3. What other important thing can Samaria represent in God's strategy?
   Prejudice

4. What was the basic reason the Jews disliked the Samaritans?
   They were the physical result of the Assyrian captivity of Israel

5. In which two stories in the Bible did Jesus demonstrate overcoming the prejudice of the Jews toward the Samaritans?
   In the parable of the Good Samaritan; The woman at the well

6. Are you building relationships today with any foreigners who are near you?
   Student response

7. Do you have any plans to do a short-term mission trip to a foreign people?
   Student response

8. Do you have any specific prejudices toward any other people? If so, how can you overcome them?
Student response

CHAPTER 36
QUESTIONS ANSWER KEY

1. How has The LIFE Plan helped you in your walk with God?
Student response

2. Would you say that you are on your way to discovering God's specific purpose for your life?
Student response

3. Would you be willing to lead others through The LIFE Plan?
Student response

4. What will you do now as a result of having studied The LIFE Plan?
Student response

5. What things did you learn from The LIFE Plan that you did not know?
Student response

6. Which LIFE lessons were your favorites?
Student response

7. Would you recommend The LIFE Plan to another person?
Student response

ABOUT THE AUTHOR

Rev. Allen L. Elder is an ordained pastor serving Southern Baptist churches in his home state of South Carolina for over thirty years. His ministry focus is upon personal disciple-making in fulfilment of the Lord's great commission. Allen is a husband and the father of three sons, a United States Air Force Veteran, and has one grand-daughter. He welcomes your response to his writings. Allen can be contacted by email at allenelder@att.net.

Made in USA - Kendallville, IN
1233648_9781692345174
02.16.2021 0859